Contents

Foreword

D r. Roby Barrett's examination and study of some 200 years of the Sultanate of Oman's dynastic history is an excellent companion piece to his earlier work, *Yemen: A Different Political Paradigm in Context*. His Oman study puts into context the last four decades of the Sultanate's history to answer the question of whether Oman has changed fundamentally from a nation fraught with instability and conflict to one of peace and stability. Dr. Barrett's research focuses on the current rule of Sultan Qaboos and his approach to change, development, and modernity in a centuries-old culture that has experienced political, economic, and social upheaval throughout most of its early existence.

Dr. Barrett's analysis of Sultan Qaboos and his understanding of the roles central authority, tribalism, succession problems, religious fundamentalism, and competing internal political centers have played in Oman's history will aid today's reader in understanding the impact of fundamental change and progress along with the external trappings of modernity from a strictly Middle Eastern vantage point rather than in the Western context. Dr. Barrett writes that "Sultan Qaboos' rule is not about liberalization and democracy. In fact, authority is probably more centralized in Oman than in any other state in the Arabian Gulf and for very good reason." Barrett's analysis of modern-day Oman will help the reader avoid the pitfalls of misinterpreting the present condition on the basis of Oman's largely tumultuous past, which often featured conflict and competition for wealth and power.

Dr. Barrett puts forth a set of conclusions about the Omani experience that focuses on Sultan Qaboos' understanding of the instability of the past and difficulties of succession. Although the Sultan has no heir, he has generated a plan to avoid the succession problems of the past. Barrett points out the role of Oman's economy and the increasing stresses governments in the Gulf region now face, particularly with the prospect of declining oil revenues, increasing populations, and rapidly increasing expectations. These challenges must be considered when planning for the future. Finally, Dr. Barrett's review of the lessons to be learned from Oman's counterinsurgency experiences of the 1950s to 1980 suggest that for reasons unique to Oman these lessons are less about military operations than they are about the role of regional politics and economics.

Dr. Barrett ends by emphasizing the British "less is more" approach to counterinsurgency, coupled with a "perfect alternative leader" in Sultan Qaboos, has resulted in a successful outcome for Oman. In contrast, the U.S. with its large commitment of conventional military force has taken ownership of its wars this past decade and has become a focal point of resistance. The insights provided in Dr. Barrett's Oman study suggest that a return to a smaller special operations war might have better results for the U.S. In a solemn ending to his study, Dr. Barrett writes "in a situation where successful nation building or a conventional military victory is unlikely; a reversion to a special operations war might in fact prevent our adversaries from winning — perhaps the best result that can be achieved."

Dr. Barrett's most recent monographs, this work on Oman and his earlier study on Yemen, are bookends that will provide the SOF reader with a deep understanding of the present and historical context which has resulted in the southern Arabian region of today.

Kenneth H. Poole, Ed.D.
Director, JSOU Strategic Studies Department

About the Author

Dr. Roby C. Barrett is a senior fellow with the JSOU Strategic Studies Department. He has over 30 years of government, business, and academic experience in the Middle East and Africa. Dr. Barrett is the president of a consulting firm, specializing in technology applications and systems for national defense and security. He has extensive experience in space systems, nuclear issues, police and security systems, command and control, technology development, and weapons acquisition as they relate to both U.S. and foreign governments. The current focus of his research is strategic security issues in the Persian/Arabian Gulf, including Iran and the Arabian Peninsula. He is a former Foreign Service officer in the Middle East with a strong background in the cultural and political dynamics of historical Islamic and political development. His posting and other assignments included Tunisia, Yemen, Jordan, Lebanon, Egypt, Saudi Arabia, and the Arabian Gulf.

As a founder of the National History Center within the American Historical Association, Dr. Barrett specializes in the application of broad historical and conceptual paradigms to issues of ongoing political and military conflict and the projection of future trends. He is an adjunct scholar at the Middle East Institute (MEI) in Washington, D.C. He provides domestic and international media commentary on a range of issues from the Palestinian territories to nuclear proliferation and the challenges of Russian policy in the Middle East and North Africa. Initially trained as a Soviet and Russian specialist, Dr. Barrett brings unique insights to the regenerated competition between Russia, China, and the United States in the Middle East and Africa.

He also serves as the senior advisor to the Board of Directors of the Bilateral Arab-U.S. Chamber of Commerce, an organization whose members include major foreign and domestic petroleum companies. He is the lead panelist on Middle East and South Asian Policy. He also participates in the

Congressional Fellowship Program, American Political Science Association, and Johns Hopkins School for Advanced International Studies in Washington, D.C. He has been a featured panelist for the German Council on Foreign Relations on Middle East and Gulf Affairs. Dr. Barrett also serves as a lecturer on Gulf affairs, Iraq, and U.S. foreign policy for the Air Force Special Operations Command and in response to special requirements.

Dr. Barrett was an Eisenhower-Roberts fellow of the Eisenhower Institute in Washington D.C., a Rotary International fellow at the Russian and East European Institute at the University of Munich, and a Scottish Rite Research fellow at Oxford University. He holds a B.A. in History and Political Science from East Texas State University and an M.A. in Political Science and Russian History from Baylor University. He is a graduate of the Foreign Service Institute's intensive 2-year Arab Language and Middle East Area Studies program and the Counterterrorism Tactics course and took part in the Special Operations course. He has a Ph.D. in Middle Eastern and South Asian History from the University of Texas (UT)–Austin. Other honors include the Guittard Fellowship (Baylor), the Dora Bonham Graduate Research Grant (UT-Austin), the David Bruton Graduate Fellowship (UT-Austin), the Russian Language Scholarship (Munich), and the Falcon Award from the U.S. Air Force Academy.

As an author, Dr. Barrett's works range from books to articles on the Arab League and digital research techniques:

a. *The Greater Middle East and the Cold War: U.S. Foreign Policy under Eisenhower and Kennedy* (Palgrave Macmillan, 2007)
b. "Intervention in Iraq, 1958-1959" in *MEI Policy Briefs*, 2008
c. *The Arabian Gulf and Security Policy: The Past as Present, the Present as Future* (JSOU Press, 2009)
d. "The Aftermath of the 1958 Revolution in Iraq" in *Ultimate Adventures with Britannia* (I. B. Tauris, 2009)
e. "Gulf Security: Policies without Context" in *MEI Bulletin*, 2010
f. *Yemen: A Different Political Paradigm in Context* (JSOU Press, 2011).

His next book, *The Ministry of Interior (MOI)/SOF Interface in the Transnational Environment: SOF's Shifting Reality*, is slated to be published in 2012.

Dr. Barrett was a guest speaker at the Bahrain MOI Gulf Security Forum (2008), the SOF Conference at the opening of the King Abdullah Special Operations Training Center (Amman 2009), and the Bahrain SOF Conference

(2010). Through deployment briefings and other forums, Dr. Barrett supported numerous military units; five examples are the 5th Special Forces Group, 101st Airborne both in the U.S. and Iraq, Naval Special Warfare Command both in the U.S. and the Arabian Gulf, 4th Psychological Warfare Group, and 19th Special Forces Group.

His commentary has also appeared in the U.S., Latin American, European, and Middle East Press — for example, Voice of America English and Pakistan Services, British Broadcasting Corporation (BBC) World Service, Canadian National Broadcasting System, BBC Arabic Service, *Gulf News*, and *The National Abu Dhabi*.

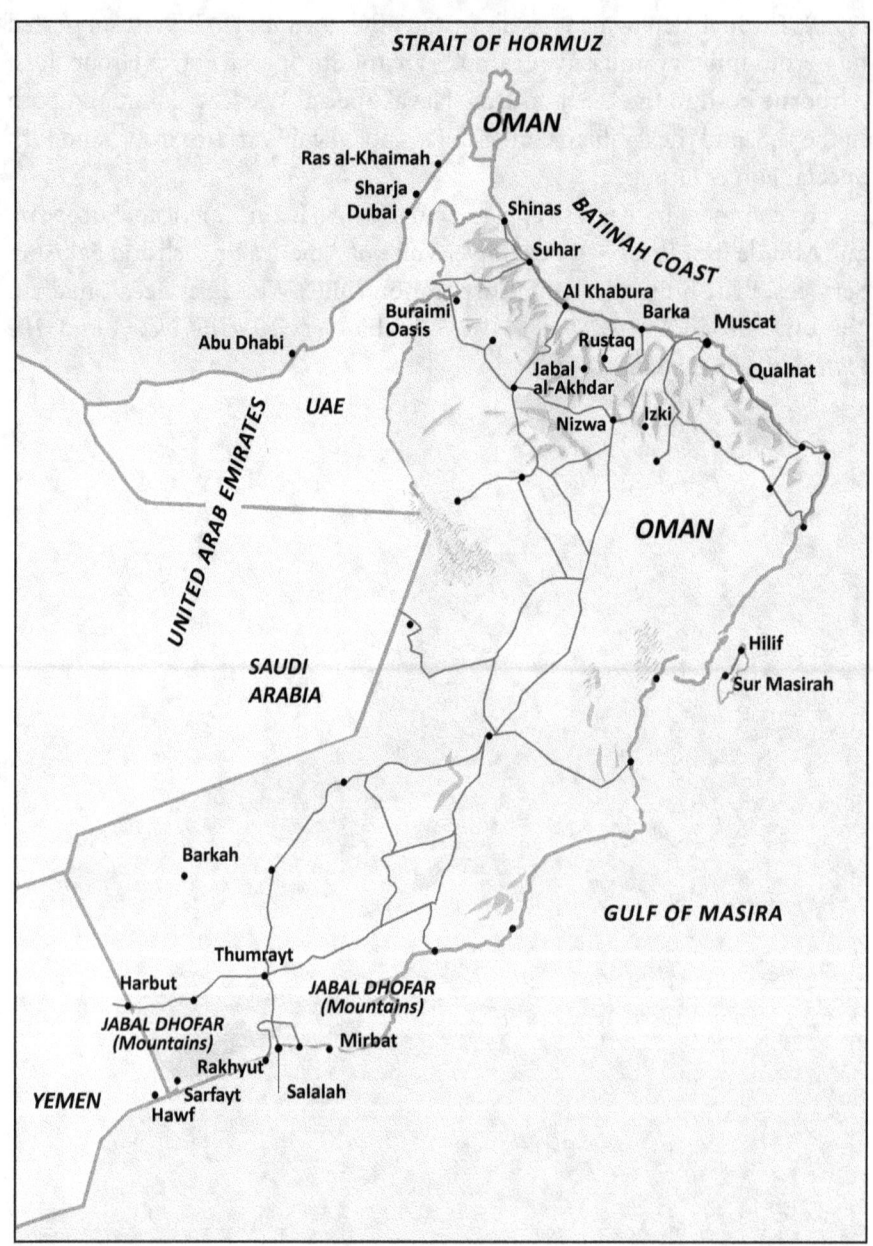

Figure 1. Oman (Created by U.S. Special Operations Command Graphics)

Oman:
The Present in the Context
of a Fractured Past

The Sultanate of Oman is a key member of the Gulf Cooperation Council and ally of the West located on the strategically critical Straits of Hormuz at the entrance to the Arabian Gulf. Contrasting sharply with its tumultuous past, its political experience of the last 40 years is often offered as a model of successful social, economic, and political development and stability. Oman is an example of how lines on a map emerge as a stable, unified nation. In addition, the ultimate success of Sultan Qaboos bin Taimur al-Sa'id (1970–present) in defeating the Dhofar insurgency in the 1970s is widely regarded as a model for counterinsurgency operations. The subsequent infrastructure and economic investment in Oman in general and in Dhofar in particular are cited as successful examples of using development as a compliment to military operations, thus removing the oxygen on which the insurgency thrived. These views are absolutely correct with regard to the last 40 years, but as recent Middle East events have demonstrated, political and cultural myopia can result in distorted analysis, which in turn can lead to unpleasant surprises. Placing too much weight on contemporary events, in this case the last 50 years, in a region where that is a historical blink of the eye can be problematic. From a policy perspective, the contemporary period, the exception, becomes the rule on which planning and strategy are based, often putting both at risk.

This short-term Western view of the past and "progress" is in sharp contrast to that of Middle Eastern cultures that define themselves based on interpretations of events that happened millennia in the past. It is difficult for outsiders to fully comprehend that the principal tie in a society is to family, clan, tribe, and region above all else and that political, economic, social, and cultural development underlie these ties.[1] A few decades of development and stability usually only provide a superficial façade behind which the old attitudes and culture are still alive and well. As a result, in the critical caldron that is the contemporary Middle East, policy at times focuses on the façade without a proper appreciation for the extremely complex political, economic, and cultural milieu behind it. The principal focus of this study is to ask that very question — in the case of a critical ally in the Arabian Gulf community: are Oman's Western allies focused on the façade or the more complex reality behind it? Is it possible that there could be a series of unpleasant surprises in store and might a more in-depth look enable the West to anticipate the unexpected and support an ally better while protecting its own interests at the same time? This study is designed to provide a snapshot of one of the more complex states of the Arabian Gulf — Oman, an introduction to the complexities that must first be understood before any other strategies and contingencies can possibly be developed. In the Middle East, there is no such thing as a one-size-fits-all strategy, plan, or operations concept — at least not an effective one.

Introduction

To attempt to explain contemporary Oman in a narrow framework outside of its deeper context is to invite, or perhaps to guarantee the lack of cultural knowledge from which to adequately address the present as well as developments in the future. This is true not only of general foreign policy but also with regard to military assistance and operational planning. In the military realm, this is more pointedly the case for Special Operations given the goal of creating operators with a detailed knowledge and understanding of the human terrain. In the Middle East, the context cannot be measured in decades and to take that view handicaps planning, operations, and strategy. A shallower perspective also tends to breed a level of complacency concerning issues that will impact the long-term stability of U.S. strategic interests and in the case of Oman that of a strategically critical U.S. ally at the entrance to the Arabian Gulf. In short, the longer view of security and stability and the coming challenges that the Sultanate will likely face must take into consideration particularly where the contemporary state resides within a far deeper historical context. In the Middle East, "the past is not dead, it is not even past." [2]

The first months of 2011 witnessed the first sustained unrest that Oman has seen in 25 years, resulting in the dismissal of several government officials and a cabinet shake-up ordered by Sultan Qaboos. [3] Is it a harbinger of things to come? In the next 15 years, Oman will likely face a transition of power from Sultan Qaboos (who rules without a direct patrilineal heir), the potential significant reduction of oil revenues to support the development, and a growing bubble of young people whose aspirations and ambitions will be ever more difficult to meet. These issues do not take into consideration that potential challenge presented by likely further fragmentation in Yemen — the same area of Yemen that fueled the Dhofar insurgency 40 years ago. Over the last 40 years, Oman's ruler has demonstrated sophistication and foresight that has produced stability, growth, and unprecedented unity, but similar periods of stability in the past driven by unusually capable rulers have later given way to instability and even chaos.

Oman may well in fact weather all of the coming challenges, but the potential exists that the stresses of the next two decades could create a situation that will require a more sophisticated, in-depth understanding of the Omani context to guide a greater level of political, economic, or military assistance than anyone at the present time anticipates. Already Saudi Arabia has offered

$10 billion in aid to boost the Omani economy. In the case of such a critical ally, it is always prudent to consider the potential for a set of less-than-optimal scenarios for the future, all of which requires a thorough understanding of the present and the historical context from which the present sprang. That is the purpose of this study; it is a bookend, if you will, to an earlier study on Yemen. In the Arabian Gulf, two states can claim unique development experiences: Yemen and Oman. Historically, with the exception of the last 40 years of stability and development in Oman, Yemen and Oman have comprised the most unstable and volatile regions in the Arabian Gulf. Sultan Qaboos' rule began in 1970, and the period of stability, development, and "progress" which has come to be associated with Oman, is usually dated from that point — hence 40 years. In reality, as we will see, the first five years of Qaboos' rule saw a military struggle coupled with a nascent program of development to gain control of Dhofar. The second five years witnessed ongoing sporadic outbreaks of anti-Sultanate activities that did not end until the withdrawal of support from the insurgency by the Peoples' Democratic Republic of Yemen (PDRY) in the early 1980s. There is a fine but important point here; Sultan Qaboos' accession in 1970 marks the beginning of Omani development, but the peace, stability, and development associated with Oman today more accurately dates from the late 1970s or early 1980s — thus 30 years from a policy point of view. To assume that 30, or even 40 years of stability has become the rule within a historical context of several millennia of conflict and instability is as naïve as it is dangerous. Yemen, which analysts and "policy experts" viewed as increasingly stable during the 1990s, has subsequently descended into internal conflict and near chaos and is a cautionary tale about superficial Western views of progress and stability in very complex and historically strife ridden societies. Oman is by no means Yemen, but a better appreciation for the complexities and problems that Oman has faced in the past and might face in different forms in the future is timely.

The competence and foresight with which Sultan Qaboos has ruled Oman — moving it from the list of underdeveloped crisis states in the 1970s to that of a success story in the first decade of the 21st century — does not change the fact that his rule has been the dramatic exception to the Omani norm. Additionally, in few instances has the stability and progress of a state been so closely associated with a single person, thus raising the question of what happens in Oman after Sultan Qaboos.[4] Viewed within the Omani historical context, the transition and its aftermath will almost certainly be far more difficult than anyone anticipates — with the exception of perhaps the Omanis themselves. As a result, this study focuses on what policymakers in general and the military in particular need to know about Oman, as basis for planning, in the event that a greater degree of involvement or level of assistance is required in the future. This study provides an essential building block for knowledgeable, sophisticated interaction with Oman and Omanis no matter what the future may bring; sophisticated interaction, operation planning, long-term strategy, stability analysis, and counterinsurgency require it. For example: Why does the succession law in Oman require that the ruler be an Ibadi from a specific branch of Al Bu Sa'id family? What are the familial implications of that requirement? What is an Ibadi? How has Ibadi Islam developed in contrast to other forms? What have been the internal forces that have fractured Oman in the past? What was the Imamate in contrast to the Sultanate? What is the relationship of Dhofar to Muscat or for that matter to the Hadramut in Yemen? The list can go on forever. This study focuses on providing the fundamentals for understanding the Omani present and considering the future.

Focusing on the last 40 years provides a woefully inadequate understanding of Oman. In recognition of this absolute fact, this paper begins in 7th century with a unique political, social, economic, religious, and cultural development that even today sets Oman apart from the rest of the Arab Gulf. Oman is an Arab Gulf State whose historical and cultural context and experience is fundamentally different from the other states of the Arabian Gulf, and a basic knowledge of those differences is critically fundamental to anyone whose responsibilities include the contemporary Sultanate. Oman's development and the conflicts that emerged from its political and social structure created an environment of almost perpetual insurrection and insurgency. As previously noted, periods of peace, stability, and prosperity as typified by the last 30 years have been few and far between. They are not the rule but are rather the exception. It is important that those charged with the responsibilities in the Gulf and planning for the *what ifs* of regional security understand and appreciate the historical fragility of the Sultanate's stability.

The multiple insurgencies in the 1950s, 1960s, and 1970s, are all outgrowths of the deep historical context. They provide useful lessons on counterinsurgency operations but more importantly, they underscore the relationship between diplomacy, development, and effective military operations as the *sine qua non* of any successful counterinsurgency effort. From the 1950s through the 1970s, Oman experienced multiple insurrections and insurgencies, all of which were difficult to suppress. The Dhofar insurgency is the best known but, in reality, the struggle between the Imamate of Oman and the Sultanate during the 1950s probably constituted the greatest immediate threat to the survival of the Muscat Sultanate. This study examines those insurgencies from the historical political and cultural contexts from which they sprang as well as the political and operational challenges and strategic difficulties that they presented. To understand and accurately place those events within the proper context, the story begins in the distant past.

"Historically, politically, and geographically, Oman has always been the most isolated part of Arabia." Sir Arnold Wilson went on to say, "Only Maskat [sic] has its eye open to the wide world."[5] Although its attributes have changed, it is this tension in politics, economics, society, and even culture that has driven the Omani paradigm and a history of competing centers of power. It is through Oman's unique history that it must be viewed and understood. Given its location on the Straits of Hormuz astride that energy lifeline from the Arabian Gulf, Oman's importance cannot be exaggerated. Oman provides multiple lessons in not only the political and military imperatives of counterinsurgency operations but also lessons in the pitfalls and challenges of providing the elusive security required for a functioning state beset by tribalism and impaired by a severely lagging social and economic development. Oman's importance to the national security of the United States requires a better understanding of its political, social, cultural, and religious experience.

This study repeatedly uses the term "legitimacy." Legitimacy, always a complicated and subject specific term, is exponentially more so when applied to Oman. Any discussion of such a complex topic in such a limited space is always an oversimplification, but a few simple guideposts can assist in framing a more sophisticated understanding. There are three basic elements to legitimacy that can best be understood by looking at Oman geographically — the Sultanate, the Imamate, and Dhofar. While separately identifiable, these elements at the same time overlap. The Sultanate is a cosmopolitan coastal society that has derived its livelihood and prosperity from participation in the Indian Ocean and global commerce for centuries. Cosmopolitanism and the British influence created a relatively tolerant, culturally inclusive society where legitimacy flowed primarily from economic prosperity and political stability. In the isolated, conservative Imamate, political legitimacy was far more closely tied to the stricter tenets of Ibadi Islam and the conservative traditions of a fractious tribal culture. Part and parcel to political legitimacy in the Imamate was the language and appearances of a much more conservative Ibadi Islamic legitimacy — the ultimate ideological weapon repeatedly used by the Imamate against the cosmopolitan sultanate. In more than 250 years, only one of the Al Bu Sa'id sultans was viewed by supporters of the traditional Imamate as worthy of becoming the Ibadi "*imam al-muslimiin.*" In a largely Sunni, ethnically African Dhofar, the situation was even more complicated — Ibadi Omanis from the North were viewed as little more than occupiers. Like the Sultanate, the culture focused on Indian Ocean trade, but historically and culturally, the Dhofaris are far closer related to the Hadramutis than to the Ibadis to the North. For the last 40 years, Sultan Qaboos has managed the "hat-trick." Through birth, born of a Dhofari mother in Salalah; outlook, the cosmopolitan progressive blending of the sultanate's view toward the sea and a progressive Western education; and predisposition, enlightened but absolute authoritarianism, he embodies legitimacy in two realms and commands legitimacy by suppressing challenges in the third. He has in effect become the irreplaceable monarch who one day will have to be replaced.

The study also provides a snapshot of policy requirements. The British and the Sultanate since the 1960s largely kept their eyes on the strategic goals while pursuing tactical objectives. There was far more commonality of policy formulation between the Foreign Office and the British Middle East Command than has been seen in recent U.S. adventures in Arabia, and this communality was driven by a significantly greater breadth and depth of knowledge. This can be in part attributed to over 200 years of the experience in the region and specifically in Oman, which undermined temptations to attempt the fundamental transformation of traditional societies. There was a minimalist approach to expectations, policy formulation, and operational execution. London supported the Sultanate, particularly in the post-World War II period, because of its interests. The Sultanate used the British in the same manner — it was a symbiotic relationship. London carefully followed the policy maxim that "less is more." In other words, the smaller the official British footprint, the better. Military intervention was kept at an absolute minimum to limit political repercussions and expenditures as well. The Dhofar rebellion subsided because London and Sultan Qaboos marshaled significant regional political, economic, and military support to deny oxygen to the rebels and remove their safe havens. The peace and stability of the last 30 years have been as much the result of diplomatic efforts, perpetual security operations and vigilance, and economic and development policies as successful military operations. Success also emanated from the Sultan's grasp of the underlying Omani historical and cultural context and an appreciation for its volatile potential. It is there that any study of Oman must begin.

The monograph has four chapters. The first provides an introduction to Omani exceptionalism — Oman's historical experience and Ibadi Islamic heritage and interpretation of the Islamic revelation are different from that of the rest of the Arabian Gulf. Perhaps, only Zaydi Yemen has a unique cultural and political experience that rivals that of Oman. "The Ibadi movement stabilized in the interior of Oman toward the latter part of the eighth century and Oman has had a unique political personality ever since."[6] Ibadi religious thought and practice served to ideologically isolate Omani cultural development.[7] This fact requires that anyone seeking an understanding of present day Oman must grasp the fundamentals of its Ibadi heritage. It also examines the rise of the Al Bu Sa'id and the interaction between the Sultanate and the Imamate from the mid-18th century to the near demise of the Sultanate in 1913. It chronicles the increasing cultural and political estrangement between the Sultanate and the Imamate, the rise of the Zanzibar Sultanate, and the increasingly assertive policy role that British India began to play in the Sultanate.

Chapter two focuses on the emergence of 'neo-Ibadism' in the early 20th century and the challenge posed by the Imamate to the legitimacy and survival of the Sultanate. It also outlines the British struggle to prop up the Sultanate through the Treaty of Sib in 1920, and its implications for the initial insurgencies of the 1950s. The study then examines the role of oil, the British Iraqi Petroleum Company (IPC), Saudi Arabia, and Arab American Oil Company (Aramco) in the tribal insurgencies of the early 1950s. This chapter reinforces the view that stability in Oman has been highly dependent on the individual ruler.

The third chapter describes the Dhofar rebellion of 1965 to 1982. It is a narrative of local grievance imbedded in an ancient past that took on the ideological colorings of the Cold War. It attempts to show the conflict in its broader context. It was far more than small Special Air Service (SAS) cadres operating against an elusive enemy. Jordanian Special Forces and Iranian Special Forces, plus air and naval forces, tipped the manpower scales in the Sultanate's favor; Saudi Arabia's decision to shift political, economic, and diplomatic support to the Sultanate ultimately undermined external support for the insurgency; and finally, the British and Qaboos removed Sultan Sa'id bin Taimur al-Sa'id at the eleventh hour to avert political collapse. All of these elements were critically important. With a broad regional consensus, substantial external support, and a sophisticated leadership from Sultan Qaboos, it took five years to subdue a region with a population of only a few hundred thousand inhabitants. An extrapolation to the current experiences in Iraq and Afghanistan is sobering.

The conclusion examines the Sultan Qaboos era within the broader context of Oman's history. Modernity and development has obscured the continuing traditional factional structure of Omani society. In Omani history, as Sultan Qaboos knows, periods of stability and prosperity often precede spectacular disintegration. As a result, the Sultan has maintained tight political and security control. Despite this, the Arab Spring of 2011 has brought the first sustained protests of the Qaboos period albeit directed not against the Sultan but against unspecified corruption in the government. Fundamental divisions still exist, exacerbated by a lack of economic opportunity. Modernity, development, and the stability of the last 30 years aside, Oman continues to be a diverse political, economic, and cultural landscape masked behind the capabilities and competence of a strong ruler — this has implications for the not too distant future.

1. The Origins of the Omani Exceptionalism and the Early Al Bu Sa'id

What makes Oman different from the rest of the Arabian Gulf? A map reveals the obvious connection with the monsoonal trading culture of the Indian Ocean and an interior isolated by desert and mountains insulating it from its Arab neighbors. In addition, the split between mountain and shore created a dichotomy in Oman's historical, economic, and cultural development. The Muscat tradition saw "Oman as a commercial maritime power, whose merchants traded from one end of the monsoon world to the other."[8] The mountain or "interior tradition" was a "closed, isolated self-sufficient community, tribal in its organization and governed by an elected Imam" according to the Ibadi Islamic tradition. Some scholars argue that the Imamate, which collapsed in the 1950s, could become a symbol of "the Gold Age of the original Muslim state" with the "mystique" of legitimacy, which if manipulated by Islamic fundamentalists could threaten Omani stability in the future.[9] Given the potency of contemporary Salafist movements, any potential for imagined purist Islamic past in Oman is worth understanding particularly if it might affect the future of a critically important area like the entrance to the Arabian Gulf.

Arab Oman and the Arrival of Islam

Oman's strategic position was particularly important to the ancient empires of Persia. Cyrus the Great, the Parthians, and later the Sassanians occupied the coastal regions. In 1st century CE, tribes from the Marib area in Yemen, under the leadership of Malik bin Fahm, migrated into Oman. While there is some debate about the exact timing, according to Hisham ibn al-Kalibi, an 8th century Arab historian, Malik defeated the Persians and established himself at Nizwa.[10] These Yemeni tribes saw themselves as Qahtani Arabs, or "pure" Arabs from southern Arabia as opposed to later arrivals, the Adnani groups from the Nejd desert in Arabia.[11] Eventually, these tribes adopted a symbiotic relationship with the Sassanian Persians through the julanda system by which they ruled on behalf of the Persians.[12] In the 7th century, Sassanian King Chosroes II's campaign to reconquer not only Oman but also Bahrain and Hadramut indicates some form of early Omani independence.[13] The Sassanian revival was short lived. Around 630 CE, the Prophet Muhammad sent a messenger, perhaps 'Amr Ibn al-'As, to Oman with a letter to the julanda, Abdul and Jayfar al-Julanda, instructing them to submit to Islam. They submitted.[14] In 632 when the Prophet died, they apparently recanted and found themselves the focus of the al-Ridda campaigns of both Abu Bakr and Caliph Omar.[15] Some credit this lapse to the Persian and Zoroastrian influence among the population, another factor setting Oman apart from its Arab neighbors.[16]

Following the death of the Prophet, disputes arose over the succession. The followers of Ali — the Shi'a or party of Ali — believed that head of the community of believers, the umma, should pass down to the most senior blood relative of the Prophet. Others in the community, most notably those of the Quraysh tribe objected and supported the more traditional consensus approach. The Muslim leadership ultimately opted for the latter approach appointing Abu Bakr as the first Caliph. He was followed in turn by Caliphs Umar and Uthman, both of whom were murdered. In 656, on the death of Uthman, Ali finally became Caliph. He faced immediate opposition from Uthman's supporters the Umayyads. At this point a third group, the Kharijites (from the Arab word *haraj*, to go out) arose. The Kharijites opposed familial succession and the Umayyads' attempts to establish their own dynasty. Initial support for Ali ended abruptly when Ali in an armed confrontation with the Umayyads submitted to Koranic arbitration. Phillips argued, "The nub of the Kharijite case was that the Quran could not be used to settle the dispute since this would involve submitting it to various interpretations, whereas "Judgement [sic] belongs to none save God; no arbitration in the religion of God." In retaliation, Caliph Ali attempted to destroy the Kharijites.[17] Unfortunately for Caliph Ali, the Kharijites managed to assassinate him. That event and the subsequent massacre of Ali's son Hussein and his followers at Karbala in 681 became the driving impetus behind the emergence of the Shi'a in Islam — but what of the Kharijites?

The Kharijite movement split. One group violently opposed Umayyad rule and another took a quietist approach.[18] Crushed by the Umayyads (661–750) and persecuted by the Abbasids (750–1258), the Kharijites fled to remote areas of North Africa and established small Kharijite states in Libya, Tunisia, and Morocco.[19] The "quietists" under Abdullah ibn Ibad al-Murri al-Tamimi emerged as a new community.[20] Taking their name from al-Tamimi, the Ibadis rejected Shi'a and Sunni orthodoxy and refused to tie the origins of their sect to any historical event.[21] For them belief was "not limited to time and place." They saw themselves as "an ancient community rooted in Quranic revelation."[22] Migrating to Oman, they made common cause with tribal elements against Umayyad attempts to expand Damascus' control.[23] The isolation of Oman provided sanctuary.[24] This combination of tribal resistance to foreign Umayyad rule and an alternate Islamic theology proved a potent combination. The Umayyads were never able to completely subdue Oman with the unconquered resistance centered on Jabal al-Akhdar — *jabal* meaning mountain in Arabic — an area key to the revolt of the 1950s.[25] Then, in 750, the Abbasids destroyed the Umayyad Caliphate in Damascus and founded a new Caliphate centered on Baghdad.

Taking advantage of the chaos, the Ibadis exploited Omani dynastic and tribal rivalries.[26] They elected their first Imam, al-Julanda bin Masud. Initially, the Omani Imamate functioned independently. However, once in control the Abbasids captured and executed the first Ibadi Imam. As Abbasid power ebbed, the Omani tribes elected and also removed imams who did not meet the standards set by the community.[27] In 793, the Yamadi, or second Imamate (793–893), was founded on a narrow tribal base and adopted the authoritarian Rustamid Ibadi School. Many of the ideas and propensities of this authoritarian, radical school of Ibadi Islamic thought arguably morphed into the neo-Ibadism of the 1950s — underscoring the potential for ideas from a distant past to resurrect themselves in a contemporary form. During this early period, the Rustamid School almost destroyed Ibadi Islam.[28] Coastal invasions by the Abbasids, the Persians, the Carmathians, and even a dynasty based in the islands off Hormuz forced the Ibadi core to remain isolated in the interior fractured by tribal wars and feuding.[29] The political and cultural development of the interior was isolated and thus different from that of the rest of Arabia. This isolation encouraged Omani exceptionalism — a unique view of themselves and their role in Islamic and Arabian Gulf politics and culture, and Oman's place in the greater Indian Ocean community.

Seafaring also set Oman apart. Centered on Sohar, north of present day Muscat, a true Indian Ocean culture developed focused more on China, India, Madagascar, and Africa than on Arabia. Omanis understood the importance of the monsoonal winds and how to use them.[30] Thus, two very different Omans developed, isolated from Arabia but linked to each other.[31] In 915, Abu al-Hasan Ali al-Masudi, the Arab historian and geographer, on his return from India and China, described his journey from Sohar to Zanzibar with a group of Omani ship owners testifying to the presence and influence of Omanis in East Africa.[32] Trade in gold and slaves also brought Ibadi Islam to places like Zanzibar and Kilwa, which as early as 975 became the trading center for East Africa.[33] By the 12th century, Omani traders flourished on the coast from Kilwa to Mogadishu, Mombasa, Malindi, Pemba, and Zanzibar.[34] This Omani trading empire roughly paralleled the growth of the Rasulid dynasty (1229–1454) that brought South Yemen under its control.[35] Like the Rasulids, the Omanis benefited from the Mongol subjugation of Iran and the Abbasid Caliphate because it shifted trade from the northern routes to the Indian Ocean.[36] Rasulid Yemen and Oman competed for trade on the African, Indian, and Southeast Asian coasts.[37]

In the 15th century, the arrival of the Portuguese devastated the prosperity of the Indian Ocean trading communities. In 1487, Vasco da Gama rounded the Cape of Good Hope. Procuring the assistance of Ahmed bin Majid, the foremost Arab navigator of the period, da Gama laid claim to much of the African coast for Portugal. In 1502, he returned with a fleet and plundered the entire coast. Portuguese tactics wrecked Omani commerce and the Muslim city-states of East Africa.[38] In 1515, Alfonso de Albuquerque occupied the Hormuz and established forts at Muscat, Qalhat, and Sohar subjugating coastal Oman.[39] The slaughter that accompanied the sack of Muscat left no room for future accommodation between the Omanis and Portuguese as the Portuguese described it, "Joao da Nova (a Portuguese commander) killed many [Omanis] well as women and children … without sparing any."[40] The Portuguese goal was total dominance in the African coast and Indian Ocean.[41] In 1538, Suleiman the Magnificent (1520–1566) sent a Red Sea expedition under Hadum Suleiman Pasha, the governor of Egypt, to secure coastal Yemen and contested the trade route to India.[42] In 1550, the Ottomans sacked Muscat and slaughtered the Portuguese garrison. Two years later, the Portuguese took it back.[43]

Political Developments in Oman

In 1620, Nasir bin Murshid of the Banu Ya'rub tribe became the first Imam of the Ya'ruba Dynasty (1620–1743). Tribally, he was a Ghafiri 'Azd. Called the Upright Ibadhi, Nasir led an aggressive campaign against the weakened Portuguese and his Omani tribal opponents. Attesting to the volatility of his 26-year rule, it was said, "no Omani 'great or small' died a natural death." In 1649, Portuguese Muscat fell to Imam Sultan bin Sayf I (1640–1680), Nasir's cousin and successor. Sultan bin Sayf II (1712–1718) turned his attention to driving the Portuguese from the African coast. He eventually cleared the Portuguese from the entire African coast north of the Mozambique Channel.[44]

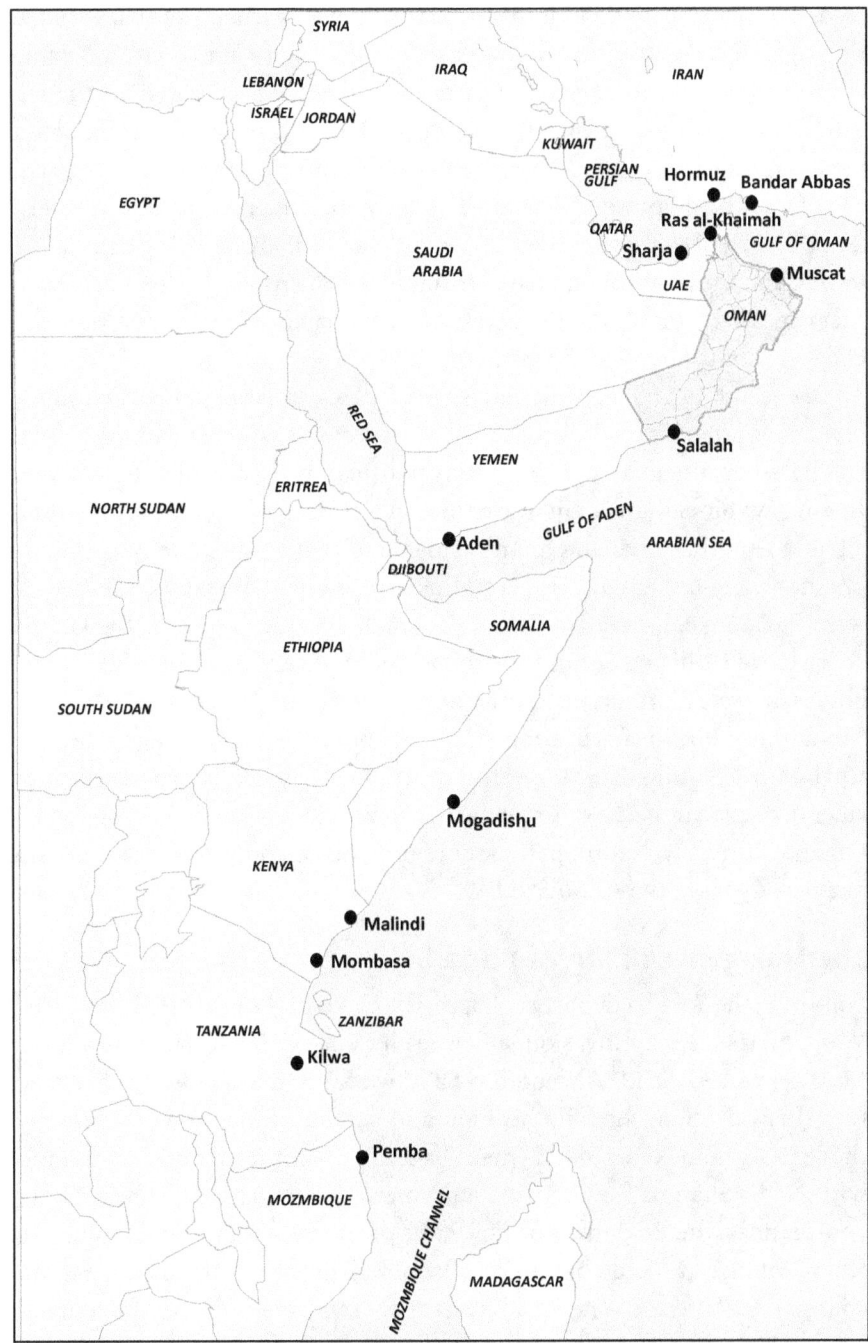

Figure 2. The extent of Omani influence and its trading empire in Africa and the Indian Ocean (Created by U.S. Special Operations Command Graphics)

Sayf II transformed Oman into a real naval power with a fleet that included one 74-gun, two 50-gun, and eighteen 12- to 32-gun ships with which he controlled the entire coast to the entrance of the Red Sea, raided Portuguese settlements in India, and in 1717 captured Bahrain from the Persian Safavids.[45] The success of the 17th and early 18th centuries represented a golden age of wealth and power. Despite all its accomplishment, the Ya'ruba Imamate collapsed because succession eventually led to a minor being next in line to rule and the political and tribal instability that ensued.[46] This was not the first time that Omani stability appeared sustainable only to have it suddenly collapse, nor would it be the last.

Between 1719 and 1727, there were five imams and even more rival candidates supported by rival ulema (religious scholar) and tribal factions. These rivalries became a fixture of Omani politics. In 1722, a dispute between Imam Sayf bin Sultan II and Muhammad bin Nasir al-Ghafiri erupted into a tribal feud that divided Oman's tribes into two groups, the Banu Ghafir or Ghafiris, and the Banu Hina or Hinawis.[47] Roughly speaking the Hinawi were the more conservative Ibadis of Yemeni (Ghatani) origin. The Ghafiri consisted of Ibadi and Sunni tribes of northern (Adnani) origin. Muhammad bin Nasir's rebellion succeeded and he declared himself Imam in 1725. Upon Muhammad bin Nasir's death in 1727, Sayf bin Sultan II once again became Imam. In 1743, still unable to control the tribes, he asked Nadir Shah, the new ruler of Persia, for help. Nadir Shah attempted another Persian occupation of Oman. Ultimately, Nadir Shah's failure provided an opportunity for the rise of a new dynasty, the Al Bu Sa'id.[48]

The Emergence of the Al Bu Sa'id

Following the Ya'ruba dynasty collapse, the chaos of the Ghafiri-Hinawi Civil War, and the Persian invasion, a new leader emerged, Ahmad bin Sa'id bin Muhammad Al-Sa'id. Ahmad bin Sa'id was an Omani commander from the Hinawi faction who built his reputation and legitimacy on opposition to the Persians and Nadir Shah. Imam Sayf bin Sultan II's temporary alliance with Nadir Shah in 1737 became a permanent occupation.[49] Nadir Shah's commander, the Beglerbeg or governor of the Fars region in Persia, Taqi Khan, captured Muscat, but his attack on Sohar where Ahmad bin Sa'id was commander faltered. When Nadir Shah sent overwhelming reinforcements, Ahmad bin Sa'id wisely negotiated an agreement whereby he remained as the

Persian governor. In 1744, he revolted and finally drove the remaining Persians from Muscat. Stories of his starving Persian prisoners at Sohar, slaughtering Persian commanders invited to feast, or putting others on ships ostensibly to return to Persia then burning the ships enhanced his reputation as someone not to be trifled with. Ahmad bin Sa'id's ferocious opposition to Persian rule enhanced his political legitimacy.[50]

In 1748, another opportunity to expand Sa'id control presented itself. The Ghafiris became disaffected with the Ya'ruba Imam and imprisoned him.[51] Ahmad bin Sa'id sent a trusted family member, Sheikh Khalfan bin Muhammad Al-Sa'id, to capture Nizwa, the traditional seat of the Imamate, and establish Al Bu Sa'id control. By defeating the Persians and eliminating the Ya'ruba Imamate, Ahmad gave the ulema little choice but to elect him Imam, the first of the Al Bu Sa'id dynasty.[52] The Al Bu Sa'id were relative unknowns before the Persian conflict and opponents used this obscurity to question the legitimacy of the family's rule. The opposition questioned Ahmad's election claiming that the opposition had been eliminated prior to the election. Later, opponents questioned the legitimacy of the electors, arguing that the title imam had been used as an honorific and not a legal Ibadi designation.[53] The Governor of Mombasa, Muhammad bin Uthman declared his independence allegedly proclaiming, "The imam has usurped Oman — I have usurped Mombasa." Agents sent by Ahmad assassinated the governor for his temerity.[54]

Ahmad bin Sa'id then took the title and energetically defended his prerogatives as Imam from his capital at al-Rustaq.[55] Oman reasserted its naval power in the Arabian Gulf and Indian Ocean challenging the naval power of the Persians and the Banu Qawasim of Sharjah and Ras al-Khaimah. As the Imam aged, he appeared to be less decisive in protecting Omani Gulf mercantile interests.[56] The actual disruption in trade may have been more perceived than real; Gulf and to some extent Indian Ocean trade were affected by the situation at Basra and Bandar Abbas, but shifting trade patterns likely made up the difference. Increased coffee trade through Mocha in Yemen and that in Javanese sugar and spices with western India through Cochin more than compensated for the disruptions in the Gulf.[57] Nevertheless, the view that Imam Ahmad was not doing enough persisted.

In 1781, Sayf bin Ahmad and Sultan bin Ahmad, two of his sons, revolted. In part tribal jealousy and the fact that their mother was from the Bani Jabir, an important Ghafiri tribe more prestigious than the Al Bu Sa'id, played a role. Angered that Ahmad had given control of al-Rustaq and Nizwa and much of the interior to his anointed successor Sa'id bin Ahmad, Sayf and Sultan captured the forts at Muscat and their half-brother Sa'id. Sa'id escaped and without a hostage, Sayf and Sultan had to flee Oman to the Baluchi coast.[58] Upon Ahmad's death in 1783, Sa'id bin Ahmad became Imam but immediately faced strong opposition. First the Ibadi ulema met in 1785 and elected Qays bin Ahmad imam. Sa'id was unable to establish his authority in the interior and focused his attention on foreign trade. He increased the share of Omani trade in the Indian Ocean and added a profitable trade in African slaves. To consolidate the slave trade, he reasserted Omani control over the Swahili Coast of East Africa and expanded trade with the French.[59]

In 1793, Sultan bin Ahmad returned to Oman and forced a family realignment that strongly favored his branch of the Al Bu Sa'id. Influence was divided among Sa'id, Qays, and Sultan. Sultan gained control of Muscat and used it to expand the trading empire from which he received sufficient revenues to maintain his fleet, his mercenary army, and the primacy of his political influence. Competing centers of power would become the norm for Al Bu Sai'd rule.[60] With the demise of the Sa'id branch, the Sultan and Qays branches emerged as the two dominant. Generally speaking, the Sultan branch controlled the "maritime state" and claiming "nominal suzerainty over the whole country." The Qays branch controlled the interior and allied with the ulema in an attempt to reassert the legitimacy of the Imamate.[61]

Despite the rough division of influence between interior and coast, Sultan bin Ahmad maintained some influence in the interior as well. In 1800, he confronted the first Wahhabi occupation of Buraimi Oasis. Defeated, he concluded a three-year truce with the Saudis. Sultan's support for the Hashemites in the Hejaz brought another Wahhabi invasion in combination with the 'Utbi of Bahrain and Kuwait and the Qawasim. Unable to counter this coalition, Sultan accepted another truce and the assignment of a Wahhabi political agent in Muscat. Yet when another Saudi offensive followed and at a unity council in Barkah, the Omanis pledged to "continue to struggle against the invaders."[62] The Wahhabis withdrew before hostilities commenced in earnest because of a succession crisis. An Iraqi Shi'a assassinated Amir Abd-al-Aziz ibn Muhammad ibn Saud (1765–1803) in the Saudi capital of Dir'iyah in retaliation for the sack of Karbala in 1801.[63] Sultan then attempted to deal with the Wahhabi's allies, particularly the Qawasim of Ras al-Khaymah and Sharjah; he was killed in 1803 in an attack upon a Qawasim warship.[64]

Converging Interests: The British and the Sultanate

The 18th century brought rising European influence on the coast and a new threatening Islamic challenge in the interior. The twin challenges put new strains on the Ibadi identity. The British victory in the Seven Years' War (1756–1763) altered their security priorities. India displaced the British East India Company (BEIC) entrepôts in the Gulf at Basra and Bandar Abbas in importance. Problems in the Gulf trade and a downturn in the coffee trade in Mocha shifted the return-on-investment equation eastward. The situation was similar for the Sultanate. Wahhabi "pirates," the emergence of the 'Utbi maritime states of Kuwait and Bahrain, Persian threats to Basra, and the activities of the Qawasim in Sharjah and Ras al-Khaymah made doing business in the Gulf less profitable.

Both Oman and the British sought to contain Gulf problems in the Gulf and stabilize the Indian Ocean trade. The French and Dutch found themselves at an increasing disadvantage to London.[65] British, and to a lesser extent Dutch, influence was further enhanced by the collapse of the Persian Safavid Empire in 1722, Nadir Shah's rule in 1747, and finally the increasing weakness in the Indian Mughal Empire. At the same time, the Sultanate's substantial trade with India and Africa while damaging to private British interests did not significantly conflict with the BEIC.[66] From the 1770s, the BEIC also received a percentage of the coffee trade routed through Muscat, and thus a direct interest in the continued safety and prosperity of Muscat. Trade also shifted away from Bandar Abbas and Basra to Muscat.[67] Rising British power caused the rulers in Muscat to attempt to balance London's influence.

In 1798 following Admiral Nelson's victory over the French at the Battle of the Nile, the BEIC, concerned that Sultan bin Ahmed was pro-French, dictated a treaty that excluded the French and Dutch from Muscat and Oman. It was the first British treaty with any Arab state and "represented England's first intervention and entrenchment in the affairs of Oman." The treaty was ratified again in 1800 and extended. Given Napoleon's attempt to enlist the Sultan in undermining British interests in the Indian Ocean, BEIC concern was understandable. The British made it clear that a failure to sign would mean that all of India would be closed to Omani commerce. Sultan not only rejected the French overture and the posting of a permanent French representative in Muscat, but he accepted a British officer as permanent resident and as his personal advisor.[68] In return, the ports and trade of India were open to Muscat and Sultan. London got what it wanted, the exclusion of the French, and Sultan got what he wanted, sanctioned access to the Indian trade. Perhaps more importantly, he gained an ally who could ensure his survival against Wahhabi, Persian, Utbi, and Qawasim aggression.

Oman and the Early Wahhabi Threat

For Omani rulers, Ibadi traditions provided them an ideological defense against both the Sunni Wahhabis and the Persian Shi'a. They equated the former to the radical Kharijites of the 7th century "who believed they had the right and obligation to kill all who disagreed with them" and absolutely rejected the latter's belief in the Alid Imamate. The Omanis referred to the Persians as "a people who are under the wrath of God." Because the core of Ibadi beliefs came from the interior, the same very conservative outlook created pronounced cleavage with the coast. The arrival of the Europeans heightened the differences. People of the interior simply could not accept the cultural menagerie of the coastal ports. Muscat was open to Europeans, Africans, and Hindus all of whom were allowed to follow their own religious practices — it was good for trade and commerce.[69] In addition, the security of Muscat and the Sultan often depended on a standing military, which tended to be African or Baluchi and more reliable than the tribal levies of the interior. Peoples of the coast and interior tend to develop antipathetically in any circumstance.[70] As the interests of Muscat and the interior diverged, Ibadi Islam became the ideological tool through which issues of legitimacy and identity were challenged, pitting the ulema and tribal interior against the commercial and "secular" interests of the coast.[71]

Following Sultan bin Ahmad's death, from 1804 to 1806, Badr bin Sayf bin Ahmed ruled as regent in Muscat for Sa'id bin Sultan bin Ahmad. At the time the Saudi Wahhabis had found allies in disaffected tribes within the Ghafiri confederation and menaced Oman from the Buraimi Oasis and the sea. In 1806, Sa'id bin Sultan assassinated Badr.[72] In 1807, Sa'id took over Sohar on the death of Qays, his uncle, putting him at odds with Qays' son Azzan. Simultaneously, the Wahhabis threatened Sa'id's regime, but were held off by some astute maneuvering and fence mending with the Ghafiri tribes. In 1813, the Saudi threat was eliminated by the Ottomans' independent Viceroy in Egypt, Muhammad Ali, whose son Ibrahim Pasha destroyed the first Saudi state.[73] Sa'id bin Sultan, also known as Sa'id the Great, ruled in his own right for 50 years as a "temporal" ruler, first adopting the title Sultan.[74]

Sa'id understood two things well: prosperity creates stability and proper management of the relationship with the British meant security. Sa'id allied himself with the British first against the Qawasim in Ras al-Khaymah and Sharjah and then against the remaining Wahhabi Emirs of the Gulf and interior.[75] Using the British as a screen for his own ambitions, he occupied Dhofar, a move that would have significant implications for Muscat in the 20th century.[76] An anonymous report in the Asiatic Journal of 1825 summed up Sultan Sa'id's use of the British:

> His government is despotic in the extreme and nothing but the protection he is supposed to receive from the British Government prevents frequent revolts. The greater part of the inland territories merely acknowledge his sovereignty, but pay no tribute; neither has he means of enforcing it. The British expedition to Beni Boo Ally, 1821, very considerably strengthened his power, and he has fully availed himself of the impression then made, to keep up a belief among his subjects, of the British Government being always ready to aid him in bringing any rebels to their duty.[77]

The ulema of the interior saw him as an illegitimate ruler, but he managed to use his relationship with the British and his political and commercial successes in East Africa to maintain his position and influence.[78]

The Sultanate and East Africa in the 19th Century

In 1828, Sa'id set out to reassert the Sultanate's control in East Africa. Leaving his son, Thuwayni as regent in Oman, he used his fleet to capture Mombasa, and in 1832, moved his capital from Muscat to Zanzibar. The British actually "encouraged" Sa'id to do this because they believed that their longer-term goals in the Indian Ocean were better served by Arab rulers than by the expense of direct British administration. As Robert Cogan, one of Prime Minister Palmerton's representatives suggested, the Sultan of Zanzibar could be "not only as a powerful political engine as regards our Eastern Possession [India] but [a source] through whose means education and morality might be introduced to an unlimited extent in … Africa."[79] From Zanzibar, Omani trade penetrated deep into Africa.[80] Like his predecessors in other dynasties, he failed to institutionalize his rule; it was totally dependent on the person of the Sultan.[81] When Sa'id died, a major conflict arose between his sons over who should rule in Zanzibar and Muscat. The British sought to avoid a fratricidal war between Sa'id's sons at all cost. The primary issue was Thuwayni and any attempt on his part to forcefully regain control of Zanzibar and undermine its efforts in the Gulf to end the slave trade, piracy, and maritime warfare.[82]

The Government of India under Viceroy John Charles Canning (1856–1858) pressured Sa'id's sons to accept arbitration. From the beginning, Canning and his advisors favored a split that left Zanzibar to Majid bin Sa'id and Muscat to Thuwayni. The British India government felt that an independent Majid would be more likely to follow their wishes regarding suppression of the slave trade than if he were subordinate to Muscat. Zanzibar was far wealthier than Muscat, and Thuwayni bitterly resented Canning's decision: "The man who is given a bone can only suck it, but he who gets the flesh eats it. I am the elder brother and I have the bone in Muscat. Majid, my junior, has the flesh in Zanzibar."[83] The actual decision was even more convoluted. Captain Robert Coghlan of the Indian Navy stated that on "legal right alone" Thuwayni was entitled to rule both Muscat and Zanzibar — exactly Thuwayni's position. However, the good Captain then concluded that "expediency" required that the two be separated because Zanzibar constituted the only center for potential political control in East Africa and because the separation of Zanzibar and

Muscat would likely do more to undermine the slave trade. Thuwayni was to receive 40,000 pounds per annum assuming he did not attempt to retake Zanzibar. On 2 April 1861, Canning awarded Zanzibar to Majid and Thuwayni was recognized as Sultan of Muscat.[84]

British lack of foresight was stunning. "Al Bu Sa'id rule in Oman in the 10 years following the Canning Award suffered more setbacks than in any period since the Wahhabis descended upon the Sultanate in the first decade of the century." After the Canning Award, if the British did not ensure Al Bu Sa'id rule then someone else would. This was not immediately apparent to the inexperienced British residents who refused support for Thuwayni against the intrigues of Qays branch, the Wahhabis at Buraimi Oasis, or from Hinawi and Ghafiri tribes. By early 1865, it appeared to the British that Faisal ibn Turki al-Saud, the Wahhabi Emir at Buraimi, intended to use an alliance with the Azzan ibn Qays to destroy both Thuwayni and Muscat. Having fought the Wahhabi threat for over 50 years, the British moved to eject the Saudis from Buraimi Oasis where they "overawed the littoral Arabs from Rass-ool-Khaimeh [Ras al-Khaimah] to Aboothabee [Abu Dhabi]" in addition to threatening the "friend and ally" of the British, the "Imam of Muscat." Colonel Lewis Pelly, the Resident for the Gulf, summed up the British position: "These Wahabees [Wahhabis] want a blow right between the eyes and they shall have it." Unfortunately for Pelly, the sultan's son Salim murdered Thuwayni. Fearing more unrest, the British found themselves supporting Salim who they considered unsavory and unreliable. Salim was overthrown in 1868 by Azzan bin Qays, who became Sultan and the elected Ibadi Imam.[85] Azzan became in the eyes of the Ibadi ulema, the only legitimate ruler of Oman in the 19th century.[86]

Legitimacy and the Al Bu Sa'id in the Late 19th Century

Perhaps the most surprising issue related to British intervention and influence in Muscat and Oman was how little the Government of India or the India Office in London actually knew about the interior of Oman. In 1872 in the preface to his translation of Ibn Ruzik's History of the Imams and Seyyids of Oman, Percy Badger wrote, "It is remarkable and by no means creditable that the British Government in India, that notwithstanding our intimate political and commercial relationship with Oman for the last century, we know actually less of that country, beyond the coast, than we do of the Lake districts of Central Africa."[87] The British did not understand the difference in ideology between the Wahhabis and the Ibadis. "To bunch the ulema of Oman with the mutawwi' simply shows total incomprehension of the Ibadis as well, indeed, as of the Wahhabi movement ... But for the refusal of British recognition, the consequent loss of the Zanzibar subsidy, and the release by the India Government of his dangerous rival Turki, it is possible that Azzan might nevertheless have surmounted all his difficulties and reduced Oman, for a time at least to the semblance of a well-ordered monarchy."[88] Robert Landon pointed out that Azzan suppressed a Ghafiri rebellion in which much of the tribe was Wahhabi.[89] "The significance of the revival of the Ibadi Imamate eluded (the British)."[90] The practical outcome was that Turki found himself besieged on the coast by the tribes of the interior and survived only with British support.[91] In 1887, the American Consul reported, "The Sultan is completely in the hand of the British representative here and generally does as he is told by that official."[92] When Faisal bin Turki al-Sa'id formally took the office of Sultan in 1888, the Al Bu Sa'id dependency on the British had become a matter of survival.[93]

To make the situation crystal clear, the British forced Sultan Faisal (1888–1913) to agree to a secret bond: "[Faisal] ... does pledge and bind himself, his heirs and successors never to cede, to sell, to mortgage or otherwise give for occupation save to the British government, the dominions of Muscat and Oman or any of their dependencies." The British position now consisted of a preeminent trade position, extraterritorial privileges, exclusion of foreign powers, the power of recognition, and subsidy control through the British agency located there and reporting to the British Government of India.[94] The Ibadi ulema considered Faisal to be "little better than a kafir, an infidel." In many respects, he was no longer viewed as Arab.[95] In the Revolution of 1895, the tribes swept into Muscat and the other coastal areas.[96] Faisal sought refuge in one of the nearby forts. Much to the chagrin of the people of Muscat and the Sultan, the British refused to intervene because it would have breached their agreement with the French.[97]

Angered by the British and looking for more reliable support, Sultan Faisal allowed the French to establish a fleet coaling station near Muscat and included French flagging of Omani vessels. The British were prohibited from searching French vessels, and behind the tricolor the Omani slave trade resumed. As one writer from the period stated, "There is no record of any slave having been set free by a French gunboat. The greatest power they exercise is by lending their flag to slaving dhows, so that it covers that nefarious traffic."[98]

Behind the French flag, the Sultan also resumed the arms trade. Afghan and Baluchi tribes were becoming better armed and as one British Resident put it, "the blood of our poor fellows lies at the door of those who have carried on this traffic."[99] The slave and the arms trade together might not have spurred the British to act but the French coaling station and Russian intrigues with the Sultan were simply too much. In 1899, the British ordered the Sultan to present himself to the commander of a British naval squadron in the harbor and sign a new treaty giving them more influence. The alternative was that he could watch the bombardment of Muscat. Faisal complied. Compromised and humiliated, in 1903, he requested permission to abdicate but was turned down by Lord George Curzon, the viceroy of India.[100] Although "personally courageous," Faisal was described as "barely literate," "apathetic," and "unbalanced" with an "unrealistic belief in his own strength and ability, intermixed with carelessness and fits of productive energy."[101] The Sultanate now thoroughly under the control of British India limped into the 20th century in a thoroughly weakened state.

Summary

In its earliest historical and cultural development, Oman was unique. Externally isolated and internally divided, periods of stability and power were often followed by precipitous descents into instability and decline. Oman's isolation and unique historical experience contributed to adoption of the Ibadi Islam and contributed to a separate political experience that pitted the Imamate against the existing centers of temporal power and religious orthodoxy — the Umayyads and the Abbasids. Thus, part of the "unique political personality" created by the "Ibadi movement" was an ongoing struggle against attempts by other Arabs to dominate the Imamate.[102] The threat from other Arabs gave Omanis a different perspective on inter-Arab relations as well. This would be another issue that would carry into the contemporary era. The Omani role in the monsoonal commerce of the Indian Ocean and the African coast and the epoch after the collapse of the Yamadi dynasty in which the Ibadis retreated into the hinterland and various foreign powers occupied the coast further enhanced the division between the coastal areas and the interior. In the 16th century, Omani commercial dominance in the Indian Ocean disappeared in the face of Portuguese pressure. The revival of the late 17th century collapsed in a succession crisis that in turn brought the great schism of 1722. The struggle between Qahtani and Adnani represented by the Hinawi and

Ghafiri tribal groupings carried forward into the contemporary era and provide additional fuel for internal political and social conflict. Omani rulers
were nothing if not pragmatic — they willingly invited foreign intervention
or assistance, as in the case of Nadir Shah, even when that intervention itself
posed a risk. Stability was fragile.

The emergence of the Al Bu Sa'id as the defenders of Oman against the
Persians was a promising beginning, but during the early period, the lack of
stable rule robbed the dynasty of legitimacy. The Sultan branch reinforced the
divide between the Omani interior and seaborne Muscat. These differences
might well have been less pronounced had it not been for increasing British
intervention. After 1861 and the Canning Award, the British were responsible
for the outcome of political events in Muscat. Stripped of Zanzibar, gunrun-
ning, and the slave trade, the Sultan of Muscat had become a British dependency. In 1871, to undermine the Qays branch in the form of Imam Azzan,
the British merely confirmed their ownership of Muscat's political future
and demolished the Ibadi legitimacy of Sultanate rulers. It ensured that two
Omans, the Imamate and Sultanate, would legally exist into the 1950s and that
a de facto social, cultural, and political split would survive well beyond that.
This divide in society also begs the question of whether 30 years of stability
can erase centuries of separate political and cultural development.

2. The Struggle for Supremacy in the Twentieth Century

In 1913, the Ghafiri and Hinawi tribes united and elected a new imam, Salim bin Rashid al-Kharusi, who declared the thoroughly discredited Sultan Faisal deposed.[103] On the surface, the issue appeared to be a straightforward internal Omani issue. A puppet of the British, Faisal's rule had been corrupt and incompetent. In reality, there was a new ideological component described by Wilkinson as neo-Ibadism. In the late 19th century, new ideas about Arab nationalism and Islam swept the Middle East. The small Ibadi communities in francophone North Africa were influenced by the writings of late 19th century Islamic reformers like Muhammad Abdu and Jamal al-Din al-Afghani in Paris, two of the leading Muslim thinkers of the age. In Oman, the "inspiration" to elect an al-Kharusi, as opposed to an Al Bu Sa'id Imam came from Abdullah bin Humaid al-Salimi, who had been influenced by the puritanical North African Ibadi reformers. "The views of Ibadism he built up fostered the ideal of the true Imamate of the orthodox community living according to the basic principles of Islam. He was also a fanatic and had no scruples about the end justifying the means." In other words, because of the political and cultural crosscurrents and ferment of the period, Ibadi Islam took a sharp fundamentalist turn, the focus of which was the end of the Sultanate and the call for a pure Islamic society.

Conservative Islamic Ideology, the Sultanate, and the British

From 1906 to 1913, al-Kharusi used the arguments of the Ibadi nadha (renaissance) and pressed for the overthrow of the Al Bu Sa'id sultanate. "Ideology and pragmatism confounded to create the last Imamate of Oman, to elect the descendant of an Imam from the Golden Age of the First destruction."[104] As Wilkinson put it, the imagery was priceless — the Al Bu Sa'id, corrupt puppets of Western infidels, replaced by the purity of the First Imamate.[105] Sheikh Isa bin Salih al-Harithi of the Bani Hina pledged his support uniting the Ghafiri and Hinawi against the British and the Sultanate. The surprised British Resident cabled New Delhi for more troops. In October 1913, Sultan Faisal died and was succeeded by his son, Taimur bin Faisal al-Sa'id, but negotiations went nowhere. Then, in January 1915, the Imam assembled a force of 3,000 for the assault on Muscat; British and Indian Army troops slaughtered them at Matrah. The assessment by the British Resident, Major L.B.H. Hayworth was bleak: "[Taimur's] government is so bad that to continue to support it in its existing condition is nothing short of immoral." Luckily, in July 1920, Imam al-Kharusi was assassinated. The new Imam, Muhammad bin Abdullah al-Khalili, was more amenable to a compromise as was Sheikh al-Harithi.[106]

On 25 September, the Treaty of Sib divided Oman between the Imamate and the Sultanate. It promised free trade, travel, and non-interference in the other's affairs.[107] The British refused to declare the Imamate independent, but the agreement promised that the Sultan "would not interfere in the internal affairs of the Imamate." The British argued, "the Sultan maintained de jure sovereignty over the whole of Oman," while acknowledging "the Omanis may regard the phrase [about non-interference] as granting them complete independence."[108] Two weeks after the signing of the treaty, the British Political Agent in Muscat, R.E.L. Wingate reported on 14 October 1920:

> Our interest has been entirely self-interested, has paid no regard to the peculiar political and social conditions of the country and its rulers, and by bribing Sultans to enforce unpalatable measures which benefitted none but ourselves and permitting them to misrule without protest has done more to alienate the interior and to prevent the Sultans from re-establishing their authority than all the rest put together.[109]

The British took over the Sultanate's administration and finance. In 1922, the British Resident for the Persian Gulf stated, "We have gradually but imperceptibly usurped the functions and authority of the State." The British created the Muscat Levy Corps, a force of 200–300 Baluchi soldiers with British officers under the Permanent Agent Muscat (PAM) and the British Government of India.[110]

In 1932, the British finally allowed Taimur to abdicate. Sa'id bin Taimur became the new Sultan. "After a succession of three weak Sultans, Sa'id appeared to be the dynamic and intelligent leader that the country needed."[111] In 1932, New Delhi forced Sultan Sa'id to acquiesce to British control. The PAM wrote to the British Viceroy: "He should, I think be given every chance to administer his State on Arab lines, and every effort should be made to free him from those relics of the past which are galling to him, while we should try, at the same time, to build up a façade of independence in the eyes of the world." There was a fundamental contradiction in making him "free to administer" behind a "façade of independence."[112]

Saudi Arabia, Oil and the Question of Frontiers

In 1938, Petroleum Development Oman (PDO) reported that the potential for oil in the Imamate did not look promising. Needing funds, Sultan Taimur contacted Standard Oil of California and the British quickly countered with a concession from the British-controlled Iraqi Petroleum Company.[113] Simultaneously another festering issue arose. By 1932, Abd-al-Aziz ibn Rahman al-Saud (Ibn Saud) had consolidated his position in Arabia and declared the Kingdom of Saudi Arabia. He had negotiated some boundary agreements with the British. In 1933, Ibn Saud granted the California-Arabian Standard Oil Company (CASCO) a concession that included "the eastern part of our Saudi Arab Kingdom, within its frontiers." At CASCO's request, the U.S. State Department attempted to determine what exactly that included.

The British claimed that the boundary was the "Blue" and "Violet" lines established in the Anglo-Turkish treaties of 1913 and 1914. These lines were of dubious legality. First, the treaties were never ratified; second they were pure colonial agreements between the British and Ottomans defining "spheres of influence" and thus arguably could not legally devolve to Ibn Saud; and lastly the lines were just that — straight lines drawn on a map without reference to anything else. The Foreign Office legal department more or less advised against using the Turkish agreements as the basis for claims. The Foreign Office persisted. Fundamentally, Saudi Arabia argued that there "never had been a frontier."[114] Saudi claims were based on the fact that tribes in the Hadramut, Buraimi, Dhofar, Oman, and Qatar paid the zakat and furnished tribal levies to Saudi Arabia. Percy Cox, the British Resident in the Gulf warned in 1926:

> Practically he (Ibn Saud) thinks that he is justified, in principle, in regaining any territory that his forefathers had a century ago, whether as territory or as a "sphere of influence." Oman was in their sphere of influence. ... I have little doubt but that in the course of time he will seek to extend his authority over the interior of "Oman."

Saudi legal arguments 30 years later quoted Cox. In 1939, the British could have negotiated the boundaries with greater leverage, but shortsightedness in both the India Office and the Foreign Office prevented anything from being done.[115]

The Buraimi Crisis

The end of the World War II ushered in a new era. In 1949, Saudi Arabia and the Arabian American Oil Company (Aramco) launched expeditions into Qatar and the Trucial States, the present day United Arab Emirates (UAE).[116] British officials complained, "Aramco at this time was more Saudi than the Saudis." Buraimi Oasis became important not because anyone believed that there was significant oil there but because the new Saudi claims included not only the tribes but also any areas where they migrated. Riyadh also argued that since Abu Dhabi and Oman were independent states and not British colonies, the matter should be negotiated between Saudi Arabia and the particular emirates with the British having no role in it. The Buraimi claim also affected Oman. In 1949, the Saudis made it clear exactly what was at issue:

> The position is that Bureimi, and the lands of Imam Khalili and their dependencies, are populated by Saudi Arabian tribes, and are not under the jurisdiction of the Sultan of Maskat, nor under the Shaikh of Abu Dhabi; nor is there any treaty between it [sic: read them] and the British Government and it is therefore unreasonable to proceed with conversations with the British Government for the delimitation of frontiers between the Saudi Arabian Kingdom and there Shaikhdoms.[117]

Because of Aramco, the British protested to the State Department, which suggested arbitration in 1950. The British "could not be certain of succeeding in a court of international law" and refused.[118]

In August 1952, Saudi Arabia occupied the Buraimi Oasis citing their former control. A British officer seconded to the Trucial Oman Levies (TOL), which was formed in 1951 by the British, described it as "blitzkrieg" stating, "A motorized column came incredibly out of the west, where there was nothing but waves of sand for six or seven hundred miles," and "before anyone knew what was happening the leader, a man named Turki bin Abdullah bin Ataishan, announced to the astonished people that he was their governor."[119] To quote member of one of the tribes whose father and grandfather had supported the Saudis: "The Saudis were very smart and had most of the tribes of the area on their side before either the British, the Sultan in Muscat or the Emir in Abu Dhabi knew what had happened."[120] The Saudis acted because Aramco appeared to have the backing of the U.S. government and secondly, the British were no longer the feared empire.[121] Surprised and cautious the British opted to blockade the Saudis at Hamsa and accept the "Stand Still Agreement" suggested by the U.S. Embassy in Jidda.[122]

Neither the Trucial States nor the Muscat government in Oman were in a position to protest; it was still left to Her Majesty's Government to protest on behalf of Oman and the Trucial States and back it up.[123] Saudi largess went beyond just Buraimi Oasis as they garnered favor with the tribes of the Omani interior as well.[124] Obviously concerned, the British reported, "The language used in communication from the Saudi Foreign Ministry suggested that their claims continued to advance; King Ibn Saud was said to own the allegiance of "all the people of Oman."[125] Ibn Saud encouraged Turki's "propaganda," "bribes," and "intimidation" activities. Wary of the U.S. role, on 6 January 1953, the British government laid out its Buraimi plan. While offering arbitration, the British backed Abu Dhabi and the Sultanate with new military deployments and a commitment "to build up the Trucial Oman Levies sufficiently to withstand Saudi infiltration and maintain our position in the long term."[126]

With the Saudis contained at Hamsa, the British then began a thorough assessment of their position and that of their allies on the Trucial Coast and in Muscat. Initially the Imam agreed to provide tribal levies to support the Sultan. He was even happier when he learned that their services would not be required because the "British Government are negotiating this matter."[127] The British were still concerned because former advisors and ministers in the Imam's government were travelling to Riyadh with "letters" from the Imam to King Saud but no Imamate shift to support the Saudis. At Hamsa, the Saudis were also busy improving their houses, collecting taxes, distributing subsidies, and equally important arranging marriages between the Saudi contingent and local families.[128] The British then assessed the position of the tribes. The list was long and detailed but provided the British a strong point of reference for understanding allegiances and splits with the tribes. The British knew who had taken Saudi identity papers and money. Turki bin Abdullah bin Ataishan, the Saudi point man in Hamsa, was very busy and effective to the point that when Riyadh called for a plebiscite in the region, the British refused because it would "confirm a situation which the Saudis had falsely and improperly created." In other words, Saudi patronage would have carried the day.[129]

With the Saudi move on Buraimi, the "live and let live" arrangement between the Sultan and the Imam became an immediate problem. The arrangement since 1920 prevented the effective extension of sultanate control into much of the interior, and the Saudis were now exploiting the situation. In an effort to elevate concern, the Eastern Department of the Foreign Ministry produced a classified assessment of the situation; they listed four reasons for this "backwater of the world" having its "tranquility … disturbed:"

> The growth of the power and wealth of Saudi Arabia and the exten-sion of Saudi territorial ambitions to Central Oman;

> The discovery of oil in Saudi Arabia and the Persian Gulf and the impact of new wealth on local tribal societies; and

> The rumored existence of oil in Central Oman.

> It is also alleged by the Sultan among others that there are signs of a change in attitude towards foreigners on the part of the Oman tribes, which may lead to a much more forthcoming policy and a disregard of the ailing Imam. The religious extremists, as personified by the Imam, have hitherto been a barrier to Saudi penetration and to the exploitation of oil by Western companies.

The British assessment went on to say:

> H.M.G.'s basic interest in the Sultan of Muscat arises from the pos-sibility of oil exploitation in his territory. His territory has little stra-tegic interest apart from this, though it affords staging posts of some value to the R.A.F., and is not geographically or climatically suitable as an alternative site for British forces in the Middle East.

After the Standstill agreement, Sultan Sa'id bin Taimur, who been prepared to fight, now refused "to take positive steps to assert his authority."Undermined once more by the British, the Sultan retired to his palace to let the British work out the problem.[130] Some believed that the Sultan never forgave the British for intervening.[131] London had once again intervened to protect its broader interests at the expense of the Sultan's prestige and independence. To underscore this, the Sultan pointedly complained to the British Resident in Muscat that the Standstill agreement created a situation in which he was losing prestige and that the Saudis should be removed during the arbitration process.[132] "The Saudis sat in Buraimi for three years, bribing and intriguing, before they were finally evicted." The Sultanate lost influence as even loyal interior tribes began to waver and go their own way, a situation that would later take years to correct.[133]

The Recapture of Buraimi and Overthrow of the Imamate

With the Saudis occupying Buraimi and rumors of new aggressive moves on the part of Saudi sympathizers and the Americans, British oil companies became concerned that the Sultan might attempt to undermine the Huqf exploration project. The British Resident believed that success with Huqf would provide some compensation for what was going on at Buraimi.[134] The Sultan in fact raised concerns about the adequacy of the Huqf force to reassert Sultanate control in the central region.[135] In 1953, the PDO recruited the Muscat and Oman Field Force to provide protection and, on 15 February 1954, the Field Force and the PDO exploration teams moved into the Janaba and Harasis region. The Imam protested to the British and Sheikh Yasir of the Janaba ordered that the white flag of the Imamate be raised in all their towns and villages. Then in May 1954, Imam Muhammad bin Abdullah al-Khalili died.[136] Sultan Sa'id bin Taimur believed that he would be the last imam, but the situation in the interior had already spun out of control. The rules in the Omani interior had changed: "the game was no longer that of Imamate against Sultanate but of the old conservative political system against the secular ambitions of leaders who sniffed the heady odor of oil politics. The old men had lost their grip and it was now the turn of the young to make their moves."[137]

On 4 May 1954, Ghalib bin 'Ali Al-Hinai (1912–2009) was elected Imam and immediately began to incite tribes to rebel. The Imam picked up more support from new tribal sheikhs. In September 1954, sheikhs loyal to the Sultan were forced to flee to British protection in Sharjah. At this point, the oil company organized an expedition with troops from the Muscat and Oman Field Force (MOFF) to reestablish Sultanate control over the promising exploration area of Fahud.[138] At this point, the new Imam declared the Imamate independent and applied for membership in the Arab League. Both the Saudis and the Egyptians, now under the open leadership of Gamal Abdul Nasser, saw this as the perfect opportunity to undermine the British and one of their puppets — the Sultan of Muscat.[139] The Imam also submitted the question of "British Acts of Aggression" to the Arab League with the Saudis and Egyptians supporting "assistance" to the Imam.[140] Both the Egyptians and the Saudis had increased the flow of money and guns to dissident tribes and the Imam so the situation was still serious.[141]

At this point, the British concluded that a solution had to be found to the situation at Buraimi. The British concern was not so much the Saudis, but rather the U.S. reaction. Washington was putting an enormous amount of pressure on the British to withdraw its troops from Suez, a situation characterized by Eisenhower as the "most dangerous" situation in the Middle East.[142] John Foster Dulles reported, "If unsolved the situation [between Britain and Egypt] will find Arab world in open and united hostility to West and in some cases receptive to Soviet aid."[143] Now, the U.S. pressured the British over Buraimi. The Foreign Office refused to compromise arguing that such a move could "prejudice" good relations with Abu Dhabi and Muscat.[144] The British would not compromise with the Saudis on Omani oil exploration.[145] Britain had too many issues of importance with the U.S. to sacrifice that relationship over the problems in Oman. As events developed in 1955, the British Resident for the Gulf in Bahrain, Bernard Burrowes, became concerned that Imam Ghalib's efforts with the Saudis and the Egyptians might result in international recognition for the Oman Imamate. Burrowes pointed out that "time may not be on his [the Sultan's] side."[146] In reply, the Foreign Office was cautious but discussed the pros and cons of taking action both in the North at Buraimi and in the central region around Nizwa.[147] British officials fretted that Sultan "was more a spectator than initiator of events" and that he "did not like to make decisions." Of course, there was another issue. When pressed about support, the British were exceedingly vague about the degree to which they were willing to support a move against either Buraimi or the Imamate itself. The Sultan was cautious because if an offensive failed it would undermine his entire position.[148]

In September 1955, the arbitration commission convened in Geneva and began to consider the issues related to the Saudi's Buraimi claim. Almost immediately, the Saudi representative began to lobby fellow commission members and offer bribes for support. The commission dissolved. Now, the British pointed to their good faith effort to negotiate at exactly the same time that the U.S. was scrambling trying to assess the implications of the Czech deal for Russian arms in Cairo and King Saud bin Abd-al-Aziz's cooperation with Nasser.[149] The overall situation blunted U.S. objections about Buraimi, and the British moved quickly. On 26 October, they used the Trucial Oman Levies to overpower the Saudis and besieged their local allies at Hamsa.[150] By nightfall, the TOL commander reported that the Saudi in charge had been wounded and 14 others captured. They were put on a British ship from Sharjah to Bahrain.[151] The next morning the TOL reported that resistance had ceased and more prisoners had been taken.[152]

On 26 October, Prime Minister Anthony Eden explained to Parliament that "hopes" for an arbitrated settlement had been "disappointed" due to "bribery and intimidation on a wide scale" by Saudi Arabia. As a result, the British government acted "to exercise its duty, which is to protect the legitimate interests of the Ruler of Abu Dhabi and the Sultan of Muscat" by restoring "their previous control of the Buraimi Oasis."[153] Saudi Arabia responded stating that it had advised the President of the United Nations' Security Council that a request would be forthcoming to discuss the Buraimi matter. Riyadh also informed the British Embassy in Jidda, "The Saudi Arabian Government do not consider that there is any difference between them and the Sultan of Muscat and Sheikh of Abu Dhabi, but the difference is between them and the British Government who have imposed their will upon these rulers in order to achieve their own private aims." The Saudis added that they rejected charges that they had "not observed the terms of the arbitration agreement" and had used "bribery and intimidation" at Buraimi. Finally, the Saudis stated that they did not accept the British version of the border.[154]

Emboldened, Sultan Sa'id immediately moved to recapture Nizwa, the spiritual if not political center of the Imamate. The plan called for a joint TOL-MOFF operation to capture Nizwa and Adam. The oil company agreed to provide aircraft and transport and support with reconnaissance. By 14 December, the MOFF had occupied both Adam and Firq with only token resistance. From Muscat, the Sultan issued a communiqué stating:

> Forces of the Sultanate of Muscat and Oman are today taking action to suppress a treasonable conspiracy against the sovereignty of the Sultan Sa'id bin Taymur. Indisputable written proofs have been found that certain disaffected Shaykhs have been plotting for some time to disrupt the Sultanate with the aid of foreign gold, arms and propaganda. To restore confidence and answer the petitions of loyal subjects and to preserve the peace such intrigues can no longer be tolerated.

In December, the Sultanate occupied Nizwa and al-Rustaq. Imam Ghalib bin 'Ali resigned and his brother Talib bin 'Ali vanished only to reappear weeks later in Saudi Arabia. Salih bin 'Isa al-Harithi also fled to Saudi Arabia.[155] On 24 December 1955, the Sultan left his palace at Salalah and traveled to Nizwa. He had finally brought the interior under the control of the Sultanate and was the first Sultan to visit the interior in over a century. In the immediate euphoria following the eviction of the Saudis and the collapse of the Imamate, most were reluctant to point out that Sultan Sa'id appeared to have no real plan to develop the country or improve the life of the people.[156] The appearance of stability in 1955 was deceiving and short lived. The internal conflicts and rivalries that had driven the revolt were still present waiting re-ignition.

The 1957 Rebellion and Saudi Arabia

In Oman, the turmoil of 1955 gave way to the peace and calm of 1956.[157] With the exception of tribal incidents that were contained, it appeared that the integration of the interior had occurred with remarkably little friction. The appearances were misleading. Imam Ghalib's brother had escaped to Saudi Arabia from whence he gained money and support to create a political movement and insurgency aimed at toppling the Sultanate. The Saudis supported the creation of the Oman Liberation Army (OLA), a force of 500 men headquartered outside Dammam.[158] They also formed a "government in exile" and opened Imamate offices in Riyadh, Damascus, Beirut, and Cairo where Sawt al-Arab radio lambasted the Sultanate and its British backers.[159] The close relationship between Nasser and the Movement for Arab Nationalists (MAN) attracted a cadre of more ideologically motivated opponents of the Sultanate and the British.[160] The calm before the storm was 1956.

By 1957, Talib bin 'Ali had completed a complex plan to raise a broad rebellion against the Sultanate. The OLA would infiltrate into the interior of Oman and link up with various tribal leaders including the venerable Saudi supporter Suleiman bin Himyar al-Nabhani and his brother Imam Ghalib. In March, the operation began. An OLA diversion along the coast brought clashes with the MOFF while the main force under Talib eventually landed on the al-Batinah Coast and made its way to the interior. Using mines and machine guns, they blocked several of the roads to the interior and gained the assistance of local tribes. He then joined up with his brother who once again took the title of Imam and declared a rebellion.[161]

The Sultan faced a real dilemma. A head-on approach seemed like a certain loser so he ordered the British officers of the Omani Regiment (OR) to take and destroy Bilad Sayt to force the Bani Riyam tribes in the area to destroy Talib's force. On 10 July, the OR was ambushed, as were reinforcements on the road behind them. Mounting casualties brought more reinforcements but no progress was made and the road ambushes in the rear were increasing in frequency and ferocity. At this point, the British tactical commander decided to abandon the Bilad Sayt operation and withdraw to Raddah. The withdrawal was difficult even before the regiment ran into multiple ambushes at Tanuf, Kamah and Nizwa. During the panicked withdrawal, an entire OR company became separated without transport and was "shattered" by point blank fire as "it passed beneath the garden walls of Nizwa." The remnants finally made it back to Raddah.[162]

The Bani Riyam had destroyed the Sultan's first line units. Considering the circumstances casualties were relatively light, a dozen dead and wounded, but more than half of the soldiers then deserted. In addition, an OR platoon holding Nizwa Fort quickly surrendered to the Imam's forces. Fearing an attack on 'Ibri, the British attempted to piece together a defense force consisting of a Northern Frontier Regiment (NFR) company, an OR platoon, and the remnants of retreating Company A of the OR. When the latter arrived, Major Malcolm Dennison, the commanding officer sent them back immediately to avoid infecting the other troops with their demoralized state. The British commander was replaced, but his replacement, who had just arrived, surveyed the mess, resigned on the spot and left Oman.[163] It was a disaster.

Appearances can be deceiving. The situation had gone from peaceful to a full-blown crisis in a matter of weeks underscoring the volatility of Oman's human terrain. On 16 July, the Sultan made a formal request for assistance to the British consul-general saying among other things:

> You have full knowledge of the situation which has developed at Nizwa and I feel that the time has now come when I must request for the maximum military and air support which our friend HBM's Government can give in these circumstances, as on those past occasions which have so cemented our friendship and which I bear lasting gratitude.[164]

The events of the summer of 1957 clearly demonstrated that the Sultan's sovereignty and control of the Oman interior was an illusion. On 18 July, in London the British chiefs of staff ordered the commander of British Forces in the Arabian Peninsula to secure Buraimi and forestall another Saudi surprise like 1952. They then ordered the Royal Air Force (RAF) to launch rocket and machine-gun attacks on a couple of the occupied forts to gain breathing space for a further buildup of forces. By 1 August, fresh ground forces were arriving. During the buildup, Imam Ghalib sent a message to the Sultan stating that he had only restored the historical situation between the Imamate and the Sultanate and that both he and the British needed to keep their forces out of his territory. In the meantime, the Sultan had gained the support of several of the tribes, which added more than 1,000 irregulars to the Muscat Regiment's planned advance through the Sama'il Gap in Hajjar Mountains, a key passage into the interior.[165]

The operational plan was straightforward. The Carter Force under Lieutenant Colonel Stewart Carter of the TOS (formerly the TOL) would advance from Fahud and take Nizwa. A second column, the Haugh Force commanded by Lieutenant Colonel Frank Haugh, was to move through the Hajjar Mountains at the Sama'il Gap into the interior. The entire operation was under the command of a regular British officer, Brigadier J.A.R. Robertson. On 5 August, the Carter force began pushing their way toward Nizwa. 'Izz and Raddah fell almost without a shot being fired. Resistance at Firq was stiff but overcome with air support by attacking rebels in the open and destroying the Tanuf fort. During the operation, British units were used for the more difficult maneuvers like a night climb to high ground on Jabal Firq to outflank the rebels below. Then, TOS units were moved forward with air support to take positions. By 12 August, the British and Sultan were once again in control of Nizwa. The fort at Birkat al-Mawz was the last to fall. The Sultan then ordered that all of the forts and towers in the area be destroyed, particularly those strong points belonging to Suleiman bin Himyar. On 15 August, Sayyid Ahmad bin Ibrahim, the Sultan's Minister of the Interior, arrived in Nizwa and began the arrest of key rebels and the reorganization of local government and oil exploration parties moved back into the area.[166]

Jabal al-Akhdar

The restoration of Sultan Sa'id's control had been relatively straightforward, but the insurgency was not over. The British and the Sultan had hoped to capture the leaders of the rebellion, but by 30 August it had become apparent that Imam Ghalib, Talib, Suleiman bin Himyar, and others had managed to escape to the Jabal al-Akhdar region. Jabal al-Akhdar (the Green Mountain) was a serious military challenge.[167] It was a "sheer limestone massif between forty and fifty miles in length and twenty miles wide." Honeycombed with caves, the mountain consisted of a plateau at 6,000 feet surrounded by peaks that reached 10,000 feet. The only approaches were through narrow mountain trails with steep, easily-defended sides, the perfect defensive position.

For the remainder of 1957, the Sultan's forces and their British officers probed at the mountain. The lack of casualties among the Sultan's forces indicated a real lack of enthusiasm for the task at hand but, in their defense, it was a daunting assignment.[168] Blockading the mountain was totally ineffective. The rebels received supplies on a regular basis and mounted operations against the British and the Sultan's forces. There was "non-stop road-mining" initially using small American and eventually graduating to large anti-tank mines. The weapons were smuggled via the Batinah Coast into the mountains. At one point, Sheikh Salih bin 'Isa managed to smuggle an entire truckload of mortars, anti-aircraft machine guns, mines, radios, and ammunition to the top of the mountain.[169]

The current political situation was unacceptable. In December 1957, the British concluded that neither massive bombing nor the introduction of British troops was a viable approach. They decided that only a top-to-bottom reorganization of the military and civil administration of the Sultanate could prevent a reoccurrence of the unhappy events of past year. Lastly, London pressured the Sultan to come to an agreement with Suleiman bin Himyar and the Bani Riyam tribe allowing them to remain at Jabal al-Akhdar if they expelled both the Imam and his brother Talib. The problem was that the British did not really have control of their client, the Sultan. In a familiar counterinsurgency dilemma, the Sultan countered that a deal with Himyar was only possible if the pressure on the insurgents was such that they would acquiesce to terms acceptable to the government. The Sultan told the British Permanent Representative for the Persian Gulf (PRPG) that the pressure had not reached that point.[170]

With the two large Bani Riyam and Bani Hani tribes supporting the insurrection, other tribes in the region refused to commit decisively before they knew the winner. In early 1958, word arrived that a large force of Omanis and others, perhaps as many as 2,000, were training under Egyptian officers at Dammam in Saudi Arabia and that they were equipped with vehicles capable of crossing the Rub al-Khali. It now became imperative that the Sultan's force be reorganized and made capable of dealing with the Jabal al-Akhdar situation before this new force could be brought into action. Following a visit in January 1958, Julian Amery, the Under-Secretary for War, reported that the Sultan's forces could not drive the rebels from Jabal al-Akhdar, the blockade was ineffective, negotiations were not going anywhere, and the government's authority was weakening.[171]

Still wanting a "painless solution," the British resorted to long-range shelling, more persistent rocket and bombing attacks, and a propaganda campaign. Nothing worked. Interdiction became more difficult as the people in the countryside concluded that the rebels would ultimately win. The toll on British officers and non-British enlisted men continued to rise. In retaliation for mortar attacks, the British had authorized attacks on livestock and canals in an attempt to make the mountain uninhabitable.[172] The British now believed that they were up against 100 Saudi-trained Omanis and about 600 fighters from the Bani Riyam tribe. They believed that Saudis were handling the mortars and radios with Egyptian trained operators.[173] Rather than getting weaker, the insurgent attacks were becoming bolder. On 3 August, a Foreign Office assessment showed alarm and growing frustration with the Sultan: "The Political Resident in Bahrain confirms recent reports that the situation in Oman is far worse than had been supposed and suggests some means of dealing with it. ... The political resident ... urged on him [The Sultan] the need for some political action to supplement our and his military efforts. The Sultan tended to pooh-pooh the whole story. If he cannot even now be convinced of the existence of an emergency, there will be a major crisis in our relations with him."[174]

As for the Sultanate, the British concluded a treaty of support in early 1958. Colonel Waterfield became the equivalent of the Sultan's minister of defense and Colonel David Smiley became Commander, Sultan's Armed Forces (CSAF). Smiley's initial assessment was "gloomy." The insurgents had more money to buy tribal support, heavy mines, and mortars, and reinforcements continued to arrive despite the blockade. In addition, most of the tribal leaders were sitting on the fence awaiting a decisive outcome. Negotiations failed and by November 1958, a British working group recommended that a total program of reconciliation, economic investment and training for the SAF be the core of a new program to retake the interior. The British position had hardened. Events around the region, including the Baghdad coup of July 1958, required the British to show resolve or risk losing their interests in the Gulf. Reluctantly, the British concluded that Jabal al-Akhdar had to be captured or that H.M.G had to completely reconsider its position in Oman.[175]

At this point, Special Air Service (SAS) units returning from Malaysia were diverted for a reconnaissance of the mountain. For the SAS, the Jabal al-Akhdar problem was a great opportunity to prove their continuing value. After discarding various plans, SAS concluded that they needed a new approach up the mountain. The four main routes, Wadi Halfayn, Wadi Tanuf, Wadi Kamah, and Wadi Bani Kharus, were well known and well guarded. A new route could not be scouted to the top because the rebels would learn of it and block it. Patrolling and air attacks kept the pressure on the rebels and the rebels' attention focused on the known avenues of advance.[176] Masked by diversionary attacks, on 26 January, the real assault began with a climb over a series of peaks to the "bridge" on the cliff and then to the high ground above the Imamate forces. Rebel units resisted then melted away. Other regular British troops and SAF units quickly joined the SAS. They located the abandoned cave that served as the Imam's headquarters. On 30 January, Colonel Smiley traveled by helicopter to the mountain to inspect the captured equipment and stores, but none of the rebel leaders or hardcore combatants were captured. They apparently slipped down the Wadi Halfayn and bribed or intimidated local leaders who allowed them to escape.[177] In the 10 weeks of operations in Oman, the SAS had three killed and four wounded. They claimed 52 insurgents killed. Most important, they ended the stalemate at Jabal al-Akhdar that threatened to undermine Sultan Sa'id and the British position in the region.[178]

The events of 1957–1959 also assisted the Sultanate. Many of the devout ulema, who had supported the Imamate, were troubled by the compromises of Imam Ghalib with the absolute ideological enemies of Ibadi Islam. As the spiritual and temporal leader of his people, his prime duties were to guide the community rightly and defend it against its enemies. He was the *imam al-muslimiin* who could not recognize a higher authority or compromise with other beliefs and ideologies, and yet, Ghalib had appealed to the UN, portrayed interior Oman as an instrument of revolutionary nationalism, declared his faith in "Arab socialism," and talked about "solidarity" with regimes as removed from Oman as Communist China. Imam Ghalib's actions had undermined the institution.[179] The rebels continued to receive support from radical Arab states and they continued their subversive activities including road mining and acts of sabotage after 1959. By 1960, the British had concluded that there was only a very low probability that the OLA or Oman Revolutionary Movement (ORM) could mount any campaign at all in Oman.[180]

Summary

Among the lessons learned from the British and Omani experience between 1910 and 1960 is that of client dependency. During the 19th century, British intervention and insistence on control in Oman created a situation in which London in the 20th century simply could not extricate itself either politically or militarily, nor could the Sultanate develop its own indigenous capabilities. The British always sought the solution that required the least investment no matter the longer-term implications. The Treaty of Sib in 1920 turned out to be a bargain. It created a de facto, dual-state solution for Oman that was recognized both by the Sultan and the Imam for over three decades. However, when oil exploration and Saudi claims changed the equation, another period of instability ensued. In the 1950s, nothing had changed; the Sultanate could not survive without direct British support. Virtually any threat, no matter how small quickly became a threat to the survival of the Sultanate, a testament to the volatility of Omani society and the cleavages that had existed for millennia. Apparently quiescent revolts and opposition to Muscat simmered just below the surface awaiting a catalyst or an opportunity to reappear. Perhaps the most significant indicator of the fundamental weakness of the Sultanate was the experience of 1957. After what appeared to be a total victory in 1955, Talib bin 'Ali returned, reclaiming the Imamate for his brother Ghalib and crushing the Sultanate's armed forces in the process. At any of these junctures had the British not been present the Sultanate would have collapsed. Groups were always willing to revolt if the moment appeared right. The situation in 1960 underscores this; even as traditional Ibadi Oman continued its simmering struggle, the third Oman — Dhofar — an area distinct from the other two would erupt in revolt.

3. The Dhofar Insurgency

This chapter examines the Dhofar rebellion from three perspectives: Dhofar itself and Sultanate policies; Dhofar as a continuation in another form of the Buraimi issue and earlier Imamate struggles; and finally, the transition of the rebellion into a Cold War proxy-struggle. The Dhofar rebellion grew out of the fundamental political, social, and sectarian differences between Dhofar, the southwestern-most province in Oman, and the rest of Oman and the Sultanate. The Dhofaris tend to be Sunni as opposed to Ibadi and speak a local language that is closer to highland versions of the ancient Semitic languages spoken in Yemen than to Omani Arabic.[181] The demographics of Dhofar are extremely complex but tribally, they can be loosely divided into two main groups, the al-Kathir tribes who occupy the plains and the al-Qara tribes who like their upland Yemeni cousins are fundamentally a warrior, mountain people.[182] Culturally and historically, Dhofar and the Hadramut have had more in common with each other than either have with Sana'a or Muscat. In addition, Dhofar was a relatively late addition to the Sultanate; conquered by Said the Great in the early 19th century, it was only formally added to the Sultanate in 1876.[183] Despite that fact that Sultan Sa'id bin Taimur designated Salalah on the Dhofari coast as his capital, he treated Dhofar as a personal fief. Administratively it was totally separate from Oman proper, and the Sultan ruled it capriciously through its traditional tribal leaders. This transformed Dhofar into a tinder box awaiting the spark.

Rebuffed at Buraimi by the British and Jabal al-Akhdar, the Saudis looked for another opportunity to undermine the Sultan and the British. Crown Prince Feisal, as Minister of Foreign Affairs and later King, had taken the occupation of Buraimi personally.[184] The Dhofar insurgency formed a bridge between the traditional dynastic and tribal rivalries to conflicts clothed in the ideological trappings of pan-Arab socialism, Nasserism, and the Cold War. Local and regional issues drove the conflict but, the insurgency was ultimately sustained by the support of radical Arab nationalist states and eventually the emergence of a Chinese and Soviet client state in southern Yemen. As long as states bordering Oman provided support for the insurgency, it could be suppressed but not defeated. The Imamate was a case in point. Defeated in 1955 and 1958, Imamate attacks and diplomatic maneuvering continued for almost a decade because of Riyadh's support and willingness to serve as a conduit for others like Egypt, Iraq, and even Kuwait to provide support. Once the conflict in Oman became a Cold War struggle between the Soviets and the Chinese, the traditional regimes withdrew their support and shifted it to the Sultanate, providing Muscat a less complicated regional situation and an improved chance of defeating it.

Oman, Dhofar, and the Regional Political Context 1958–1967

Because of the British, Oman and the Aden Protectorate were two things on which Nasser and Feisal agreed. Saudi Arabia's territorial ambitions vis-à-vis Buraimi and the Omani interior and its anti-British policies merged into a cooperative venture with those of Nasser, the secular Arab nationalist who wanted to expand Egypt's influence in the Arabian Gulf. At this point another opportunity arose to undermine the Sultan and British. The Sultan's policies in Dhofar created a crisis.[185] After Jabal al-Akhdar, Sultan Sa'id retreated to his palace at Salalah. The Sultan had unified Oman but ironically like the Imams he had no intention of instituting reforms and modernizing the country. He wanted to keep Oman. This policy was particularly oppressive with regard to the policies in Dhofar, his personal fiefdom.

> The people of Dhofar, the [UN] Committee was told, were treated by the Sultan as slaves. He was cruel and imposed many arbitrary restrictions on the people. They could not travel outside; they were not permitted to build houses; food could only be bought in one walled market where the quantity that could be bought was fixed; and they were not allowed to import or export goods. Further, there was no work in Dhofar, no schools, no hospital, no economic life, no equality and no right to participate in politics.

The Sultan was "impermeable" to outside advice, taking the position "if Oman's little rulers [tribal sheikhs who maintained order] were all right then so is Oman."[186] The Sultan was totally out of touch.

Dhofaris, who wanted to better themselves, left Dhofar for jobs in the Gulf and Saudi Arabia and joined the Trucial Omani Scouts (TOS). Those who left returned with new ideas around which opposition began to coalesce. There were six basic groups: The Arab Nationalist' Movement (ANM), the Dhofar Benevolent Society (DBS), the Dhofar Soldiers' Organization (DSO), the Hizb al-Zhaf (Party of the Advance), al-Kaff al Aswad (The Black Palm), and finally Musallim bin Nufal and the Bayt Kathir tribal grouping. Dhofaris became associated with the ANM while living in Cairo and Iraq or through their Ba'thist contacts in Kuwait. The DBS was a charitable organization that eventually morphed into a cover organization for ANM members in Kuwait. Disaffected Dhofari soldiers composed most of the DSO. The Hizb al-Zhaf was associated with Dhofaris in the TOS. The Black Palm was a *khuddam* (Dhofaris of African decent) organization that melded into the Dhofar Liberation Front (DLF). Musallim bin Nufal bin Sharfan al-Kathari was the driving force that unified the disparate opposition groups into the DLF.[187] Musallim, a *jabili* (tribal person from the mountains), had served in the small Dhofar Force (DF), the only pre-1960 defense force in Dhofar. After his dismissal, he was arrested several times for causing trouble. By early 1963, he had been involved in several attacks on oil exploration, military, and Sultanate personnel. Around 1964, on a trip to Saudi Arabia, he met Talib bin 'Ali al-Hinai, the younger brother of Imam Ghalib and the leader of the 1957 to 1959 campaign that culminated at Jabal al-Akhdar. Talib bin 'Ali provided Musallim with arms, ammunition, and perhaps some training for his Dhofari recruits. In 1964, the Saudi al-Murrah tribe provided vehicles and support to cross the Rub al-Khali. Musallim opened an expanded campaign of mine laying, sniping, and even mortar attacks. Sultanate Armed Forces (SAF) units had no luck in locating him. Then more reports of Dhofari insurgents transiting the Rub al-Khali in Saudi-supplied Dodge Power Wagons was followed by more ominous news that Iranian naval units had intercepted a dhow loaded with 50 Dhofaris and weapons in route from their training facilities in Iraq to Oman.[188] Eventually the Iranians turned the Dhofaris over to the British and the Sultan who questioned them further and, in June 1965, 40 *jabilis* and townspeople in Salalah were arrested. The threat was real—a replay of 1957?[189]

On 1 June 1965, at Hamarin in the Wadi al-Kabir in central Dhofar, the opposition groups met and created an 18-man executive committee to coordinate an armed struggle against the Sultanate. The Dhofar Liberation Front (DLF) issued a communiqué on 9 June.[190] The "political manifesto" called for:

a. The poor classes, farmers, workers, soldiers and revolutionary intellectuals will form the backbone of the organization.
b. The imperialist presence will be destroyed in all its forms—military, economic, and political.
c. The hireline [sic] regime under its ruler, Said bin Taymour will be destroyed.[191]

For credibility, the committee ordered three immediate strikes against the British and the Sultan targeting an oil company truck, an RAF vehicle, and a military camp at al-Raysut was attacked.[192]

In 1965, the SAF estimated that approximately 300 insurgents were operating in three groups. Muhammad bin Suhayl bin Sayrat al-'Amri's group operated around Mirbat and Taqah; Salim Amr bin Ghanim bin Shams Bayt Samhan were in the area around Wadi Jardum; and finally, Salim bin Bakhi bin Zaydan al-Bar'ami focused on the Wadi Nahiz. Dhofar Liberation Army (DLA) reinforcements continued to arrive. It was not clear that the Sultan grasped the seriousness of the situation, but the British officers did. They feared a Dhofar Force mutiny and a major propaganda victory for the rebels.[193]

During the early period, relations between their Arab sponsors constituted the biggest problem. By early 1966, Saudi Arabia, and to a lesser degree Kuwait, were rethinking their cooperation with Egypt and Iraq. Then, in late 1966, Riyadh blocked the movement of 120 Dhofaris trained in Iraq through the Rub al-Khali. With the Yemen Civil War now at its height and Egyptian aircraft bombing Saudi border towns, King Feisal refused the DLF assistance as long as it received support from Nasser. Because of decreasing British control, far eastern Yemen had become the new focal point for transit and aid to the DLF.[194] The National Front (NF) in Yemen had become an Egyptian client. By early 1967, Saudi funding for the DLF had ceased and, in December the Peoples' Republic of South Yemen (PRSY) emerged under the control of the Egyptian-backed NF.[195]

Other realignments brewed as well. The British frustration with the Sultan was growing. Sultan Sa'id was outliving his usefulness. In January 1966, writing to the PRPG William Luce, the British Consul in Muscat, Bill Carden stated: "The next five years will be a contest with the rebels and their friends trying to oust the Sultan and us before he can consolidate his position by expenditure of oil revenues." In fact, it became a race between the rebels and the British to see who could oust the Sultan first.[196] In 1966 a stalemate arose and the British, if not the Sultan Sa'id, realized that something decisive must be done or Dhofar would be lost with unpredictable results for the rest of Oman. In April, a DLF assassination attempt almost succeeded. At a military camp in Salalah, a staff sergeant and a soldier fired, missing the Sultan. The British immediately brought in an NFR company and regained control, but not before *jabili* and Bayt al-Kathir soldiers deserted taking their rifles with them. The subsequent investigation revealed that the DF had been thoroughly penetrated by the rebels since 1962. The Sultan now recognized that security concerns about the DF were justified. Despite harassing attacks by the DLF and a lack of men, equipment, and supplies for the SAF, the SAF made what appeared to be significant progress in 1967.[197] This appearance of progress by the SAF and its British officers would shortly vanish in another round of regional political shifts that would invigorate the insurgency.

The Insurgency Begins in Ernest 1967–1970

In December 1967, the Yemeni National Front came to power as the British withdrew from Aden and the Protectorates. The border areas of southern Yemen had provided a haven for the rebels but British control subjected the area to raids and retaliation. With the NF, the DLF now had a safe-haven from which they could recruit, arm, and resupply. In addition, powerful transmitters of Radio Aden and the *Sawt al-Arab* in Cairo intensified the propaganda campaign: "Throw off the harness of British Imperialism. Take the wealth that is yours but is stolen by the Sultan."[198] More importantly, the PRSY and the DLF became Arabian proxies in the global struggle between the West and the Communist Bloc. They were the only game on the Arabian Peninsula for Beijing and Moscow receiving more attention and support than their size or potential probably warranted.

In September 1968, the DLF held its second Congress and adopted the language of the class struggle; they called for the pursuit of "scientific socialism" and "organized revolutionary violence." It was an "attempt to escalate the local tribal revolt into an ideological movement with mass popular support throughout the Gulf." The movement also needed a new more ambitious, politically correct name; it became the Popular Front for the Liberation of the Occupied Arabian Gulf (PFLOAG). Because of the unwieldy acronym, it became the Front or *jabha*.[199] The military wing became the Peoples' Liberation Army (PLA) following the Chinese model.[200] The members of the old DLF including Musallim bin Nufal of the Dhofar Arab Youth Organization and Yousef al-Alawi of the Dhofar Charitable Association left. The new General Secretary was Muhammad Ahmed al-Ghassani. He headed a General Command Council with 25 members of which only three were previous members of the DLF command structure. Just as the National Liberation Front (NLF), the former Yemen NF, attempted to undermine tribal culture and politics in South Yemen, the PFLOAG sought to crush tribal influence by collectivization through "committees for agriculture" and "model farms."

Those who resisted these programs or the edicts of the "Committee for the Solution of Popular Problems" (tribal disputes) faced "economic sanctions" or were simply shot by "PFLOAG Commissars." Military and economic support came from the PRSY, the Peoples' Front for the Liberation of Palestine (PFLP), China, North Korea, and the Soviet Union. Oman entered the Cold War.[201]

The PRSY had an immediate impact on the battlefield. The Sultanate's relative control in 1967 quickly turned into a full-blown insurrection in 1968. Complicating matters, the British announcement that they intended to withdraw from their military commitments "east of Suez" by 1971 brought consternation to the Arab Gulf emirates. Given Dhofar and continuing problems in the Jabal al-Akhdar region, the British withdrawal appeared to be a harbinger of disaster for the Sultanate. The Soviet Union and other radical groups reinvigorated their support for liberation movements in the Gulf expecting that the end of a British presence coupled with the emirates lacking capabilities for defense and basic government administration constituted a real opportunity to "liberate" the Gulf.

As the firefights and ambushes increased in 1968, so did the evidence of significantly increased aid via the PRSY. In April in the western area near Wadi Sayq, two PRSY soldiers were captured. By May, firefights with insurgents increasingly involved men in khakis as opposed to tribal garb. In June, NFR units killed an insurgent in Wadi Janin who was carrying a Chinese version of a Kalashnikov replete with a Mao Zedong badge and another badge carrying the seal of the Dhofar Liberation Front in Arabic. SAF resupply had become a nightmare. Operations simply grounded to a halt because of the lack of logistical and transport capabilities. While the SAF struggled, tribal irregulars loyal to Sultan attempted to maintain security in the villages and to keep roads open with mixed success. Even the RAF base at Salalah came under mortar attack.[202]

Numbers varied but the SAF assessment placed the number of Maoist, "hardcore regulars" at 200–300 with another 1,000 irregulars. However, well-informed independent sources put the number at 2,000 PFLOAG fighters in organized units and another 3,000 irregulars who could be called upon for operations. In 1970, Dhofar's entire population was only 60,000 — approximately half of that population lived in and around Salalah. Thus, in the area of operation, PFLOAG forces likely equaled 15–20 percent of the population. The Front headquarters in Hawf, PRSY divided Dhofar into four sectors (*wahdah*) containing two or three paramilitary units (*firqah*). Each unit had a commander, a deputy commander, and a political officer. The latter managed non-military issues and could remove a commander and order executions. The units were intentionally mixed and rotated to remove tribal allegiances and replace them with ideological ones. Hardcore units were equipped with mortars, machine guns, howitzers, and recoilless rifles. By 1970, the weapons were increasingly Chinese copies of Soviet weapons. The Front's build up during the late 1960s outstripped that of the SAF forcing the Sultan's military and its British officers into increasingly defensive postures. The Front outnumbered the SAF and was better armed.[203]

By 1969, Front units were able to harass SAF positions almost at will and, by focusing on transportation bottlenecks in the *wadis* and mountains, they severely hindered both troop movements and resupply. By July 1970, the government was on its heels. Salalah was a fortified armed camp and everything outside the wire was hostile territory. The Front controlled Jabal Dhofar and the border areas back 24 kilometers to Salalah itself. Lack of water and the problems in evacuating casualties turned most SAF operations into operational nightmares. Many of the population centers could only be reached by air because the Front controlled the roads, day or night. The new CSAF, Brigadier John Graham, cited the total lack of any political, economic, or intelligence plan to undermine the Front's control in the countryside. [204] The Front was effectively in control of about two thirds of Dhofar and rebel activities were about to spread.[205]

In the North, the Popular Revolutionary Movement of Oman and the Arab Gulf, the Revolutionary Vanguard of the Students of Oman and the Arab Gulf, and the organization of Arab Soldiers of Oman (former TOS soldiers) merged into the National Democratic Front for the Liberation of Oman and the Arabian Gulf (NDFLOAG). This organization targeted northern Oman, Jabal al-Akhdar, and al-Sharqiyah region, none of which had been totally pacified. The new revolutionary government in Baghdad headed by the Iraqi Ba'ath Party supported it.[206] This was an Iraqi attempt to assert its leadership in the Arab Gulf. Just as the government's fortunes were reaching their nadir in Dhofar, the NDFLOAG launched an "urban campaign" in June 1970. Hoping to bring a quick government collapse, the NDFLOAG targeted Izki and Nizwa, former centers of resistance to the Sultan's government. Due to poor planning, several of the NDFLOAG insurgents were captured including four members of the Central Committee. The NDFLOAG then resorted to desperate tactics including forced collectivization and the routine use of torture and execution. In turn, this resulted in a counter-revolutionary movement in the North largely driven by the tribes and resulting in a significant number of defections from the NDFLOAG.[207] Despite the failure, the offensive underscored the dire position in which the government now found itself facing multiple threats with insufficient resources.

The attacks in the North were the last straw for both the British and for those in the government that believed Sultan Sa'id bin Taymur's policies would prove the undoing of the Sultanate. Some members of the Al Bu Sa'id had been calling for the removal of the Sultan for some time. Sayyid Tariq bin Taymur Al-Sa'id had had contacts within the Peoples' Organization for the Liberation of Oman (POLO) in Iraq and had formed an alliance with the Imam's brother, Talib bin 'Ali. Tariq clearly believed that only the removal of Sultan Sa'id and his own accession to the throne could save the Sultanate.[208] Qaboos bin Sa'id, the Sultan's only son, had concluded the same thing with regard to himself, "cooped up in his father's palace like a medieval prisoner."[209] Fearing any outside influence, Sultan Sa'id placed Qaboos under virtual house arrest in Salalah after his return from abroad.[210] The NDFLOAG operation in the North brought the issue of Sultan Sa'id to a head.

In Muscat, all the key British officers knew about the plan to tell the local Salalah commander to support Qaboos. On 23 July, in Salalah, Qaboos and a group of armed *askaris* surrounded the palace and cut its communications. Some local sheikhs entered the palace to arrest Sultan Sa'id while Qaboos informed the local SAF commander who then drove 10 *askaris* to the palace. With an Arab Lieutenant in charge, the detachment cornered the Sultan in the palace. Fearing execution, the Sultan insisted on surrendering to Lieutenant Colonel Turnill. In the confusion, Sultan Sa'id had managed to shoot himself in the foot, literally and metaphorically. With the palace secure, Qaboos' personal secretary arrived, presented Sa'id with a document of abdication, and the Sultan signed.[211] The Sultan was treated for his wound and put on a RAF plane to London. Those involved kept the news of the coup secret for three days in order to make certain that Sa'id was safely under wraps in London and to inform Sayyid Tariq bin Taymur that Qaboos was now Sultan.[212]

Qaboos' Accession and a Reinvigorated Sultanate

On 25 July, a general announcement was made. Four days later, the new Sultan arrived in Muscat to participate in a formal accession ceremony. On 2 August, the exiled former Sultan's brother, Sayyid Tariq bin Taymur, returned to Oman after eight years of exile. Qaboos immediately toured the country beginning with Nizwa, PDO facilities, al-Rustaq, al-Sib and various SAF sites. The new sultan did not receive all with open arms. Sheikh Ahmad bin Muhammad al-Harithi, the paramount sheikh (*tamima*) of the al-Hirth tribe and the single most powerful tribal figure in Oman, was detained and then sent to India for medical treatment. When he returned in April 1971, he was kept in isolation at Salalah as a political prisoner.[213] At the time, Major General Tony Jeapes was an SAS lieutenant colonel teaching at the army staff college at Chamberley. He was very much involved in the British military's counterinsurgency thinking and strategy formulation. He stated:

> It was quite evident that Qaboos had seized power in the nick of time, but the question was whether or not he would be allowed time for his plans to mature. Two things were clear: first, that the answer to the insurgency lay in civil development, and second, that the answer had to be found by the Omanis themselves. Vietnam had shown that there is no future for a foreign army of intervention in a national revolutionary war. None the less, the new Sultan needed all the friends that he had.[214]

The British were focused on maintaining the smallest military footprint possible and winning the war through the use of proxies. In a xenophobic land, less was more — a good point to remember.

With the new Sultan, the counterinsurgency strategy shifted dramatically. "The adoo's ideological strength had been founded on the grievances that the Dhofaris had endured under Qaboos' father. Qaboos removed those grievances and this was not lost on the people of Dhofar."[215] Qaboos granted amnesty to many political prisoners and ended Dhofar's isolation. The DF was incorporated into the regular SAF and Dhofar's status was elevated to a province. Next came a new military strategy. Over time, the military would establish a line from the sea to the Rub al-Khali to interdict the Front's main supply route and strong points on the escarpment overlooking the PRSY border. The SAF took Simba (Sarfayt) and fortified the position so that the Baluchi soldiers could defend it from any conceivable assault. It also became the hard point against which the Front would unsuccessfully expend much of their resources. The SAF also began a psychological operations campaign. Defections jumped from one in September 1970 to 100 in March 1971. Musallim bin Nufal al-Kathiri, the original rebel, argued that there was no longer a justification for rebellion since the new Sultan was willing to provide more than Dhofaris had originally sought. The government's propaganda campaign played heavily on Islamic themes and contrasted them with anti-religious tenets of the Front.[216]

The change at the palace prompted the British to make an offer of greater assistance and a new SAS plan calling for them to: (1) create an intelligence system; (2) encourage defectors and use them against the Front; (3) drill water wells and provide veterinary assistance to the jabilis; (4) provide medical assistance to the *jabilis* and towns; and (5) institute a psychological opera-tions campaign. The new plan would incorporate all of these elements and the SAS would take responsibility for recruiting, training, and leading *firqahs* of former Front fighters against their former comrades. Although the Front was very active, the SAF was invigorated by the new Sultan in Muscat and a real strategy. Phase I had succeeded — the Front had not won. Phase II called for the preparation of solid offensive operations. Phase III was to take the fight onto the Jabal, and the last phase was to consolidate the ground gained by extending the control of the government to the reclaimed areas.[217]

Initially, the Front viewed Qaboos in the same light as his father; however, they soon began to realize that this was an entirely different breed of leader. First, the primary original motivation for revolt, the rule of Sultan Sa'id, had been removed, undermining the allegiance of many fighters. Second, the doctrinaire Marxist approach alienated even more. Then there was the simple fact that the morale, arms, and aggressiveness of the SAF meant they were much more likely to be killed or captured. The Front had made progress on the Jabal. Tribal feuding was significantly reduced; women actually played a role as fighters; there was more equality among groups and for the first time intermarriage between groups was not only allowed but encouraged; however, the insecurity created by the new policies of the government caused the more doctrinaire hardcore elements to overreact. Severe punishments and executions became more frequent. "In later years, the Front's terrorist tactics against its own population were cited as a major factor in why it was unable to win the war at a time when nearly everything seemed to be in its favour." The Front was also grappling with new problems. It had moved from small unit operations to almost conventional efforts with large units. The larger units drew much more attention from the Sultanate of Oman Air Force's (SOAF) strike aircraft and created logistics issues.[218]

At its third Congress held in Rakhyut in western Dhofar, the PFLOAG issued a new 29-point plan that endorsed "other means of struggle in urban and rural areas" in addition to its previous stance that a "protracted, stubborn peoples' struggle is the only way to liberate the Gulf."[219] In December 1971, NDFLOAG merged into the PFLOAG.[220] The movement also shifted its objectives and changed its name to the Front for the Liberation of Oman and the Arabian Gulf, the challenging acronym was the same. Attempting to broaden its base, the new goal became a "national democratic revolution" as opposed to a "socialist revolution." It called for an end to illiteracy, slavery, tribalism, and oppression of women. The party once again opened its ranks to non-Marxist members.[221] Under Sultan Qaboos, the government had regained the political initiative.

The SAF regained the military initiative as well. In October 1971, Operation Jaguar gained control of the eastern part of the Jabal from which future offensives would be launched. Perhaps most important, support had improved. There was more artillery, the training programs improved SAF capabilities, and helicopters were introduced. With helicopters, resupply on the mountain was simple and operations that were previously limited to a few days could go on for months. The SAF was no longer in fixed predictable positions but could move and strike at will.[222] From the perspective of the insurgents, something had to be done to change the momentum; perhaps the most difficult task of all in insurgency or counterinsurgency operations is to entertain and to implement shifts in tactics and policies in anticipation of future changes when current tactics seem to be working. In effect, the PFLOAG with the upper hand in 1970 missed the significance of the change at the top and lacked a contingency plan for changed circumstances.

The Front Attempts to Regain the Initiative — 1972

1972 began with a series of aggressive SAF operations in both Dhofar and Oman proper. In Dhofar, Operation Leopard was intended to seal the border. Recognizing the threat, the Front and its PDRY allies made a series of diversionary attacks across central and eastern Dhofar in an attempt to draw troops and support away from Leopard. In the border areas, the PDRY initiated a troop build up particularly at Harbut, while SAF deployed in depth to prevent the Front from outflanking their border efforts through the Rub al-Khali. In an attempt to regain the initiative, the Front and PDRY went on the offensive launching a full-scale attack on the fort opposite Harbut. Reinforcements and SOAF airstrikes extricated the small garrison, but the fort had become a symbol of the Sultan's authority. At this point, British advisors disagreed on strategy. The Front had utterly destroyed the fort using satchel charges. The Sultan's Defense Secretary, Colonel Hugh Oldman, advised the Sultan to abandon it; he then departed on a trip to Pakistan. When asked his opinion, the Commander of the SAF, Brigadier Graham tactfully suggested that reoccupation of the fort and retaliation against the PDRY positions might be more productive. The Sultan ordered 48 hours of operations by the SOAF against PDRY and Front personnel on the other side of the border that destroyed supply warehouses and troop positions around Hawf the PFLOAG headquarters. There was some fear of PDRY retaliation with Mig-17s but that never occurred. When the PDRY complained to the Arab League and the UN, the Sultan replied that he welcomed UN and Arab League observers on the border and would pay for them to actually witness what was going on. The offer was never acted upon resulting in a further loss of broader Arab support for the PDRY.[223]

To get relief on the border in early 1972, the Front attempted to escalate the war in the North; it failed. In addition, Dhofar's monsoonal season, rain, fog, and low clouds, no longer forced SAF to abandon the mountains. Helicopters made the difference. Now the Front lost its seasonal respite from SAF operations. SAF's new year-round capability in the mountains brought a strategy crisis for the Front.[224] The Front decided on another offensive operation modeled on the Tet Offensive that had so demoralized the Americans in Vietnam — a military disaster for the Viet Cong — it had turned into a political triumph for Hanoi. The Front plan planned an attack on Mirbat. The idea was to penetrate the town, execute local leaders, tribal sheikhs, and other government supporters, and then disappear. The Front would demonstrate to the population that the Sultanate could not protect them.

At Mirbat, the Front faced a mix of Dhofar Gendarmerie (DG), *Firqah* Salahadin, and local tribal irregulars. The Firqah Salahadin was commanded by the former deputy commander of the Front's eastern sector, Salim Mubarak, and was a hardcore unit of Front defectors.[225] The Mirbat defense had a 22SAS British Army Training Team of nine men, in total around 100 men, one piece of artillery (a WWII vintage 25-pounder) with an assortment of rifles and light machine guns. The rebels massed about 250 men armed with recoilless rifles, mortars, and heavy and light machine guns, rocket propelled grenades, and Kalashnikovs. Their plan was to overrun two small outlying positions and then launch a surprise attack on the Mirbat fort with two columns while two other columns attacked the town itself from different directions. The insurgents believed that surprise coupled with lack of air support due to low monsoonal clouds would provide the edge that they needed to overwhelm the defenders.[226]

Tony Jeapes in *SAS Secret War* muses about the "what ifs" that must have been in the mind of the Front commander as they waited in the early hours of 19 July to launch their attack. The decoy had worked and other SAF units in the area were chasing diversions. "With luck," Mirbat would be an easy nut to crack.[227] A sudden thunderstorm that made the *wadis* impassable and delayed the attack for several hours was a harbinger of things to come. There were two outposts on Jebel Ali, a hill that guarded the approach to Mirbat. Nine DG officers manned them, four in one and five in the other. The Front's guides overwhelmed the first position quickly but resistance from the second position alerted the defenders, who from the Mirbat fort held off the attackers with machine guns, mortars and, in a separate position, the vintage 25-pounder firing over open sights. Other units repelled the assault group approaching the town along the beach. The last rebel column was ambushed by one of the local *firqah* commanders, Muhammad Sa'id al-Amri, who decoyed them into the open by waving a Kalashnikov over his head and then opened fire at close range driving them back. Having depended on the monsoon to provide protection from air attack, the British Strikemasters diving through the cloud cover at dangerously low-levels to attack their positions was a shock.[228] There was more bad news for the attackers. A new SAS squadron had just arrived in Salalah and was preparing to test fire their weapons on the range prior to deployment on the border with the PDRY. The squadron was in battle dress, fully armed, and loaded with ammunition. SOAF helicopters went to the range, picked them up and flew them to Mirbat, adding two 10-man SAS teams to the defense force. Already reeling from the unexpectedly stiff defense, the Front assault columns were now caught between the "anvil" of SAS units and the "hammer" of the government *firqah* defenders. Smashed, the Front force now focused on just survival.[229]

Mirbat shattered the confidence of the Front's young fighters. To restore discipline, Front commissars resorted to executions, which in turn led to fighting between insurgent groups and more defections. "Apart from boosting Sultanate morale and seriously depleting insurgent ranks, the defeat gave the front a crushing psychological blow. It was never again able to mount such a large-scale attack." With the central region secure, it allowed more government and SAS resources to deploy in the mountains and western sector facing the PDRY.[230]

Consolidation of Control and Foreign Assistance 1972–1975

The ability of the SAF to operate in mountains during the monsoon of 1972 and Mirbat allowed for the consolidation of control. The Midway or Thumrayt roads were opened and SAF control on the jabal expanded. Reinforcements from Jordan, Iran, and Britain allowed the SAF to become more aggressive along the border including an unauthorized raid 80 miles inside the PDRY border. Desperate, the Front once again attempted to shift the fight into the North. Solid security work led to the arrests of dozens of Front members in al-Rustaq, al-Batinah, and Nizwa. In addition, United Arab Emirate (UAE) security units arrested additional Front members on their side of the border and turned them over to the government in Muscat. Of 76 arrested, a dozen were executed and the remainder imprisoned.[231]

In late 1972, the new SAF commander, Major General Tim Creasey had significant advantages over the past. There were Iranian and Jordanian Special Forces and support units in the field with the SAF. In addition, the spike in oil prices following the 1973 oil embargo had provided Sultan Qaboos with financial resources heretofore unseen. Creasey streamlined the Ministry of Defense and supported the formation of a National Defense Council headed by Qaboos. The Council under Sultan Qaboos' leadership continued to push for expanded military operations and the political effort to "isolate the insurgents" and "win the hearts and minds." For the first time since the insurrection began, the SAF dominated the mountains for the entire 1973 monsoon season. In addition, deployment of the Imperial Iranian Task Force opened Thumrayt road and allowed Civil Action Teams to expand government development projects.[232]

Despite government successes, hardcore Front units continued to be a threat with Aden taking a more direct role. Abd-al-Aziz al-Qadi, the secretary general, made all the major decisions from Aden. The PFLOAG's fourth National Congress in January 1974 decided to target the western sectors and Sarfayt and requested more direct support from the PDRY. In addition to weapons and safe haven, the PDRY began to provide direct tactical support, medical care, security for staging areas, additional training, and even flew cross-border bombing missions periodically. By 1975, there were indications that the PDRY had as many as 500 of its own troops operating in western Dhofar and the Soviets, Iraq, Libya, and Palestinian organizations had supplanted the Chinese and Egyptians as the major Front supporters.[233] To combat this, the Sultanate now had 500 British military personnel. The Jordanians provided a battalion of Jordanian Special Forces to support offensive operations and the Shah of Iran eventually introduced Iranian SOF units in 1973, C-130 transports, interceptor aircraft, and antiaircraft units in late 1974. Operationally Iranian results were mixed, but the manpower and equipment freed SAF units for offensive operations.

The Iranian presence also created a beneficial byproduct. The presence of Iranian/Persian Shi'a troops and air units in Oman alarmed Riyadh. Now, the Saudis also began to provide equipment and financial, and perhaps most importantly, diplomatic support to the Sultanate.[234] Riyadh worked to induce Aden to stop supporting the rebels. The Iranian presence in Oman alarmed the Saudis as much or more than that of the leftists in South Yemen. From 1972 to

1979, the Saudis tried to convince Sultan Qaboos to remove the Shah's troops. The last Iranian soldiers did not leave Oman until after the 1979 revolution.[235]

By December 1974, the Popular Front for the Liberation of Oman (PFLO) could claim control only in the Shirshitti area of caves northeast of Rakhyut. The SAF now believed that it had the resources necessary to expel them from this base of operations and destroy their logistical structure in the area. The original plan had called for the Iranians to capture the caves, but resistance proved too strong. In January 1975, the two Iranian battalions managed to capture Rakhyut and effectively isolate the cave complex. The final push began in late October 1975. A helicopter assault placed Iranian SOF on the ridge above the caves, which were heavily bombarded by Iranian warships. In November 1975, the remaining Front commanders withdrew to the PDRY.[236] Although the western sector was clear of insurgents, small hit-and-run attacks continued in the central region with occasional artillery attacks along the border; nonetheless, the situation allowed Sultan Qaboos to declare the Dhofar rebellion suppressed.

In reality, the Sultan's declaration did not end the conflict, but the PFLO now faced a difficult situation. There were recriminations about their failure. The PDRY also came under considerable pressure. Saudi Arabia was offering inducements including aid and recognition in return for ending support to rebels in Oman and the Yemen Arab Republic. On 9 March 1976, the day that Saudi Arabia established relations with the PDRY, the Aden government ordered an end to cross border activities. Frustrations within the Front sparked internal disputes in which the PDRY army had to intervene. Small scale incidents continued in the interior and occasional border incidents continued for years, but the end of aggressive PDRY support for the Front effectively ended the Dhofar rebellion.[237]

Summary

The Dhofar rebellion was as much a political as a military victory. The fact remains that but for a series of political events, some totally fortuitous and unpredictable, the insurgency might have succeeded or at least forced a compromise solution that left the Sultanate, Oman, and Dhofar truncated. What were those political events? Foremost, the coup against Sultan Sa'id bin Taymur Al-Sa'id and the immediate availability of a first-rate replacement in the person of Sultan Qaboos was the absolute key to ultimate success. No amount of military effort could have legitimized or propped up Sultan Sa'id.

If the political leadership is corrupt and unstable, the chances for success are virtually nil. Each for their own reasons, the British and Qaboos decided that if the Sultanate and the gains of the 1950s were to be preserved, then Sultan Sa'id had to go. After much delay, the British acted to support Qaboos and lance the political boil of leadership. That event alone split the Front between the traditionalists and the ideological radicals and reduced its effectiveness by an order of magnitude.

The second issue is that of an insurgent safe haven. Counterinsurgency has little chance of success as long as the rebels can operate with impunity from a safe haven. In the case of Oman, first the Saudis and then the PDRY provided a base of support and operations from which the rebellions could have continued indefinitely. In the late 1950s and early 1960s, radical Arab nationalism provided the Kingdom with a smokescreen and allies behind which they could pursue their frustrated territorial ambitions vis-à-vis the British and their clients in the region. The collapse of Saudi relations with Nasser's Egypt in the late 1950s and then the Yemen civil war brought a growing awareness in Riyadh that radical secular movements no matter what their ideology were a threat to the Kingdom. Frustrated territorial issues with Buraimi and the Omani Imamate aside, King Feisal recognized that historical disputes and ambitions notwithstanding, the Sultanate was preferable to the potential existential threat of the radical regimes, and finally Iranian involvement in Oman sealed the issue. Strategically, hardly anything could be worse in Saudi Arabia's view than a Gulf Arab state seeking security through a relationship with Iran and the presence of Iranian troops on the Peninsula. The Kingdom shifted from an adversary to significant supporter of the Sultanate. In the end, Saudi pressure deprived the Front of its safe haven.

From a military point of view, the British always sought the minimalist approach. The British were obsessed with economically supporting the war effort. Contract officers were hired by the Sultan and the involvement of the regular British army peaked at around 500. London and the Sultan found proxies. The Jordanians supplied trainers and combat troops. The Iranians in 1975 and 1976 had between 5,000 to 8,000 troops on the ground plus a large Imperial Iranian Air Force contingent. The Sultan, the British and the United States encouraged the Shah's view that Oman was the perfect opportunity for him to play his role as the "Policeman of the Persian Gulf." The Front complained that they were defeated not by Omanis but by a Sultanate army composed of British, Baluchis, Pakistanis, and Indians and by large contingents of Iranians and Jordanians.[238] There is some truth to that argument but it was the Sultan of Oman with his British advisors that engineered that situation and defeated the Front and its backers. In addition, the British presence was never large enough that they became the issue as has often been the case as other Western powers attempted to defeat insurgencies. Then of course, the Front also had impressive backers but did not succeed.

Figure 6. A propaganda leaflet used by the Sultanate and the British to undermine the Communist Dhofar insurgents in the minds of Muslims. "God's hand destroys communism,"

This raises the final issue. The communist and socialist ideology of the insurgents coupled with the tactics that they employed — executions and torture — to maintain loyalty and extract information left them vulnerable to the Sultanate's pro-Islamic propaganda campaign. Unlike the struggle with the Imamate where the Sultanate often found itself at an ideological disadvantage, the Dhofar rebellion allowed the Muscat government to use the politically potent ideological weapon of Islam against its communist and socialist enemies. In effect, the government was riding the social and cultural mainstream of the region and the insurgents were the *kafirs* or infidels. Sultan Qaboos convincingly painted the Front as foreign and anti-Islamic using culture and ideology to undermine his opponents. It is difficult to conduct a successful counterinsurgency campaign from the wrong side of culture and ideology and the bigger the footprint, the more difficult the task of staying on the right side of both.

4. Conclusion: Oman, Counterinsurgency, Legitimacy, and the Future

As opposed to focusing on the last 40 years, this study places the Sultanate of Oman within a deeper more complex context by examining the last two centuries, the period of Al Bu Sa'id rule and the unique identity provided by the Ibadi Islamic tradition. It is through that deeper more complex context that the implications of contemporary period, the last 50 years or so, can be accurately assessed and projections for the future made. Developments — political, economic, social, and military/security — since 1980 have been predicated on Sultan Qaboos and his close advisors understanding the role that unique features in Oman's historical and cultural experience contributed to the insurgencies of the 1950s, 1960s, and 1970s. The Omani policies of the last 40 years reflect a fundamental grasp of the political, social, economic, and cultural frictions that have comprised the Omani landscape since the 18th century. That appreciation for the deeper context, as much as anything else, explains how 250 years of conflict and instability have in the last four decades been ameliorated or suppressed — but in all likelihood not eliminated.

This history of instability raises a series of important questions about change, development, and modernity. First, and perhaps foremost, is the question of whether or not the last 40 years fundamentally changed Oman. Do potential cultural and societal conflicts exist? What does the immediate political landscape look like in terms of the deeper historical context? To what degree have security and stability been associated with the person of the ruler as opposed to long-term political and social institutions? How concerned is the current ruler and the security establishment with stability and control issues? After 30 years of peace and stability in Oman, there is a tendency to forget what the previous 12 centuries looked like. In fact, many analysts probably have a sketchy knowledge of the past and would be hard put to explain the relationships between critical events even in the immediate past. A hazy understanding could be further complicated by a tendency to view political and global developments in superficial Western terms of progress. In the Middle East, fundamental change or progress and the external trappings of modernity are completely separate things. In the case of Oman, confusing the two begs a misinterpretation of the present and potentially grossly inaccurate projections about the future.

If the discussion is limited to only the Al Bu Sa'id period, a unified Oman has only existed best case since 1920 and worst case since 1975. For the previous 200 years or so the Sultanate often hung by a thread to the coast with only London or British India protecting its existence. The norm has been conflicted between competing centers of power in a fundamentally tribal culture where rule and influence depended on the ability and resources that a ruler could bring to bear to co-opt or intimidate different competing societal elements. This was true even within the ruling Sultan branch of the Al Bu Sa'id itself. Conflict and competition was rife from almost the beginning. With the exception of the brief rule of Imam Azzan bin Qays (1868–1871), no ruler had the potential to unify the country until Sultan Qaboos. This accomplishment would have been most problematic without oil wealth and significant outside support. In fact, the oil wealth was the driver that led to British support for the unification policies of Sultan Sa'id bin Taymur (1932–1970) in first place. Until it was apparent that the Imamate had oil, unification was simply not worth it. In the aftermath of the insurgencies of the 1950s, 1960s, and 1970s, Sultan Qaboos used his limited oil wealth adroitly to push modernization and development and political peace and stability, but the fundamental structure of society did not change. Modernity overlaid a traditional society and culture. The underlying political, economic, social, and cultural differences are likely alive and well, and require constant monitoring as evidenced by the vigilance and quick reaction by security forces to any perceived threat.

In practical terms, this historical experience suggests a set of conclusions about the Omani experience. First, the Sultan's understanding of the instability of the past and difficulties of succession, under the best of circumstances, has generated a plan for avoiding the problems of the past. Second, the role of the economy and the increasing stresses that governments in the region now face particularly with the prospect of declining oil revenues, increasing population, and more rapidly increasing expectations are challenges that no one should underestimate. Finally, there are the lessons to be learned from the counterinsurgency experiences of 1950 to 1980 — for reasons unique to Oman these lessons are less about military operations than they are about the role of regional politics and economics.

Stability, Succession, and the Centrifugal Forces

First and perhaps foremost, the Sultan Qaboos understands the role central authority, tribalism, succession problems, religious fundamentalism, and competing internal political centers played in the history of the Sultanate. His development programs and reforms of the last 40 years represent an attempt to neutralize the political, cultural, and ideological tendencies of the past twelve centuries. Sultan Qaboos' rule is not about liberalization and democracy. In fact, authority is probably more centralized in Oman than in any other state in the Arabian Gulf and for very good reason. Institutionalized stability, unity, and continuity are three commodities that have been sorely lacking in the historical development of the Sultanate. In their assessment of Oman, Allen and Rigsbee argued that "Sultan Qaboos should be viewed as much more of a status quo ruler whose actions have derived much more from reaction to internal forces than to proactive progressivism on his part."[239] The fact that the Sultan retains absolute power and that the government functions within the parameters established by Qaboos supports this interpretation; however, when viewed from within the context of Oman's historical experience, Sultan Qaboos' efforts are consistent with those of a ruler focused on the strategic security of the state. Oman's present simply cannot be divorced from its past where centrifugal forces proved to be the greatest long-term threats to the Sultanate. Even when external threats emerged, those threats found fertile ground in the political, religious, tribal, and cultural fissures in Omanis to their advantage. Sultan Qaboos' rule reflects an acute awareness of this issue. The central issue has been securing institutional and political stability and continuity and an orderly succession.

Security issues dominated the first 10 years of Sultan Qaboos' rule, but the development of political institutions was not entirely ignored. In 1981, the Sultan presented the creation of the *Majlis al-Istishari li al-Dawla* (state consultative council or SCC) as his "fulfillment of our promise and in pursuance of our policy which aims at allowing a larger measure of participation for the citizens in the economic and social plans." The operation of the SCC was carefully circumscribed by a series of limitations and procedures related to its conduct. Ultimately the SCC won the right to review social and economic legislation before it went to the Sultan for approval. In 1991, Sultan Qaboos announced the formation of *Majlis al-Shura* (consultative council); this replaced the SCC. The Majlis was proportioned on the basis of population and there was an expectation that it would eventually lead to direct elections.[240] It has not. There is a high degree of tribal representation in the Majlis even in areas that are fundamentally urban. The tribes continue to play a critical role and are described as "an essential element to promote national unity and political legitimacy."[241] This carefully monitored and controlled process of expanded political participation is designed to vent political pressure without bowing to it. Real political liberalization could, and most likely would threaten the political stability of the state. Although economically driven, recent sustained demonstrations tend to lend weight to this judgment. The Sultan knows, and is well advised, to ignore those well-meaning friends who would promote naïve ideas about liberalization and democracy at the expense of stability.

The new succession laws also clearly reflect a prudent awareness of this past. The new Basic Law passed in October 1996 came as a result of the Sultan being seriously injured in an automobile crash. Article Five states: "The system of government is a hereditary Sultanate in which succession passes to a male descendant of Sayyid Turki bin Sa'id bin Sultan." The new Sultan also must

Figure 7. Secretary of Defense Robert M. Gates is greeted by Omani Sultan Qaboos at the Bait Al Baraka Palace in Muscat, Oman, on 5 December 2010. DoD photo by Master Sgt. Jerry Morrison, U.S. Air Force. (Released)

be an Ibadi Muslim. The article goes on to state that the Sultan must be an adult, born of legitimate Muslim parents and be of "sound mind."[242] The fact that the law limits succession to the Sultan branch of the Al Bu Sa'id is understandable; however, it contains the seeds of discord that have affected competing branches of the Al Bu Sa'id for generations and potentially opens the door for an Ibadi Islamic fundamentalist argument like those that legitimized the various opposition movements and plagued the Sultanate in the 19th century and most of the 20th century. Depending on the next Sultan, the succession also has the potential to ignite opposition among Sunnis as well who are excluded from consideration. The Sultan is undoubtedly correct in his judgment that this approach offers the best chance for a smooth transition and stability; however, he is just as undoubtedly aware of the potential problems that may arise.

The process of choosing a new Sultan outlined in Article Six further underscores the complexity of succession. Sultan Qaboos has no heirs; therefore, the Basic Law states that the Ruling Family Council (RFC) shall pick a new Sultan within three days. If the RFC cannot come to an agreement, then "the Defense Council will confirm the appointment of the person designated by the Sultan in his letter to the Ruling Family Council." The Defense Council is composed of senior government and military officials appointed by Sultan Qaboos.[243] In an interview, Sultan Qaboos explained that he had written down two names in descending order and placed them in two envelopes that for security reasons are held in different regions of the country. The Defense Council is to open the envelopes and make their decision.[244] The assumption is that one of the two people on the Defense Council list will be chosen, but according to government officials, the RFC is not obligated to accept Sultan Qaboos' nominee to replace him. If they believe that another individual is more suitable then they may select him and the Defense Council is constitutionally obligated to accept him.[245] There is enormous speculation about who the Sultan has designated as his replacement. Even assuming that all goes as planned, it will be very difficult to fill Sultan Qaboos' shoes. Internal rivalries and power struggles could emerge well after the actual succession takes place. Because the Sultan has granted the constitution, he can take it away. It is a "law-based state" and the Sultan is the ultimate authority — "inviolable."[246] The Sultan's throne is a prize that ambitious individuals and factions might go to great lengths to possess.

The ultimate guarantor of the stability and, for that matter of the succession itself, will be the military and security services. In many respects, the Omani military and security organizations continue to reflect the historical Omani reality. Important regiments in the SAF continue to be made up of Baluchis while the command structure and the Omani units, of necessity, favor the northern tribes "with long military ties to the sultanate."[247] The military itself retains its highly British flavor with British officers still serving under contract. The military is strongly tied to the Sultanate through the tribal elements and families that dominate the command structure. The security services also reflect similar tribal and family ties and are critical to the ongoing stability of the government. As we have seen, the history of the Sultanate is replete with examples of rebellions that came as total surprise to the government in Muscat. Buraimi, Jabal al-Akhdar, and Dhofar fall, to one degree or another, into this category. The security services under Qaboos have been pervasive and hypersensitive to the potential for an internal threat. During the last 20 years, there have been periodic arrests of individuals believed to be plotting against the government, most notably in 1994, 2002, and 2005. Then there have been the recent demonstrations on the heels of the Arab Spring. This aggressive vigilance is another strong indication of the Sultan's awareness that the underlying fissures in Omani society still exist and that if the unity of the state is to be maintained then the regime must take seriously any indication that active opposition could coalesce and grow. Actions against potential opposition groups while not officially publicized have been very public; a warning that opposition to the government will not be tolerated.[248] In that regard, some Western officials who have represented the plan as "fool proof" should take into consideration the recent and the more distant past.[249] The unity and cohesion that Sultan Qaboos' rule has brought over the last 40 years tends to obscure the historical norm, namely centuries of internal conflict and division. Qaboos' rule by virtually any parameter has been exceptional in every sense of the word and should not blind Oman's allies to a far more complicated and unstable historical context.

Oman and Economic Development

The economy is the second dominant consideration for continued stability and the most important elements were a small population and petroleum. At the time of the insurgencies, the Omani population was around 600,000 simplifying both the counterinsurgency task and economic development issues.

Post-1970, Omani oil production while modest by Gulf standards was sufficient to support a program of infrastructure development aimed not only at improving the lives of Omanis but also tying the country together and making governance and control less of a challenge. Roads, airports, and communication improved life in the countryside. It improved the internal cohesion and security of the state. Virtually all that has been accomplished since 1970 has been directly or indirectly funded by oil production. The promise of oil drove Sultan Sa'id bin Taymur and the British to move against the Imamate in 1955, and it was the revenue from that oil that allowed Sultan Qaboos to modernize and expand the SAF to combat the Dhofar insurgency.

Now production is declining and a 2004 survey revised the estimates of Omani reserves downward by 40 percent. If new reserves are not discovered, Oman could exhaust its current reserves within 15 years. While there is talk of gas production and the discovery of new reserves, the fact remains that the drop in oil production has come at a time when there is an inverse rise in the population. Oil is directly connected to employment. By some estimates only about 10 percent of private sector jobs are held by Omanis; this could result in a demand for even greater funding outlays from a government that is increasingly strapped for cash. "It appears that the sultanate will face a serious economic crisis in the next 10 to 15 years, or even sooner if oil prices plummet."[250] It is entirely conceivable that this potential economic crisis could occur at about the same time as the succession is taking place. This could put an enormous amount of strain on the government in Muscat.

The Sultan and Omani officials are well aware of these issues and have plans to diversify the economy including linking themselves to the petroleum security needs of other Gulf states. There are plans for pipelines to provide the emirates of the Gulf with access to the Indian Ocean. New oil and gas exploration is underway. Nevertheless, the Al Bu Sa'id could become the focus of widespread discontent should the economy falter under the pressure of declining petroleum revenues. Unless projections change, succession and sharply reduced petroleum revenues might well intersect. Given the history of instability, it would appear that a sober assessment of a worst-case scenario that links Omani economic, succession, and security issues appears to be in order. In this regard there is an additional potential aggravation; Oman and Yemen, the bookends of southern Arabia, could be simultaneously looking at sharply reduced oil revenues. Yemen is unstable enough in its own right, and the potential that unrest could spill across the border into Oman and that reduced financial security might make it difficult to counter deserves some consideration. Given the importance of Oman, it behooves the West to think in terms of what could happen as opposed to what they think or hope will happen over the next 15 years in Oman.

Counterinsurgency and Oman

In terms of counterinsurgency, Dhofar and the Omani experience is less a model than a cautionary tale. By almost any standard, the Omani insurgencies were small. The populations affected were small allowing for a much easier application of military operations to defeat insurgent forces and "soft" power initiatives to deprive the insurgencies of the oxygen of indigenous support. In addition, the presence of non-Muslim troops was small. This allowed the counterinsurgency effort to stay on the right side of the ideological divide — the Sultanate could readily use Islam to discredit the late Imamate through its association with secularist Egypt and later the Front and its socialist and communist ideology. The presence of large numbers of foreign non-Muslim troops is always a counterinsurgency complication in the Middle East and Southwest Asia. Where populations are large and the presence of foreign troops invasive, the counterinsurgency forces themselves are an issue against which the indigenous population can be rallied. In addition, in a smaller war, one piece of operational luck can have a far greater impact than any amount of luck in a larger conflict. In Dhofar, Mirbat is a prime example. Taking nothing away from the heroic performance of its defenders, fortune smiled on them and the Front never really recovered from the defeat.

There is also the issue of insurgency in a chronically conflicted political, economic, social, and cultural environment. External opponents of the Sultanate found a heterogeneous society and culture that always seemed to provide a resource for the resiliency of the insurgencies. The 1955 move by the British and the Sultanate to eject the Saudis from Buraimi and to end the Imamate appeared to have unified the country. Then, in 1957, to everyone's astonishment Talib bin 'Ali's arrival with Saudi and Egyptian support would have toppled or driven the Sultanate back to the coast had it not been for British intervention. The Jabal al-Akhdar campaign of 1958 and 1959 appeared to have ended the Saudi-Egyptian threat only to have plotting and insurgent activities continue into the early 1960s. When the Dhofar rebellion erupted, focus shifted to the South; nevertheless, when a diversion was needed, the

Front, the Egyptians, or the Iraqis could find enough followers to force the continued presence in the North of SAF units that were needed in Dhofar. Sultan Qaboos declared the Dhofar rebellion ended but problems with the Front and the PDRY persisted well into the 1980s.

There is a broader lesson to be learned here. In the tribal societies of the Middle East and Southwest Asia insurgencies arguably do not end — they mutate. Groups shift allegiances; ideology changes; outside supporters shift; but in virtually every case, underlying instability and armed resistance or the threat of it continues in one form or another. Conflict is a fundamental part of the political and social landscape of the region. There are simply not enough resources and opportunity to give all of the major groups an extended stake in society; therefore, conflicts erupt over what resources and opportunities exist.

There is another important political lesson as well. Regional political shifts and initiatives deprived the insurgencies of critical outside support and safe havens. During the 1950s and the first half of the 1960s, the successes of the Sultanate and British at Buraimi and at Jabal al-Akhdar in 1959 were insufficient to end the insurgency as long as Saudi Arabia supported it. Egypt and Iraq also played roles but Saudi support was the key. Initially, Riyadh also contributed to the Dhofar insurrection. The success of Front operations in Dhofar — and ultimately the very survival of the Front — was dependent on the safe haven provided by the PDRY. Even after Sultan Qaboos declared victory in 1975, the Front lingered on with PDRY support. The Saudis played a significant, if not key, role with the PDRY by trading recognition and aid in return for Aden ending support to the Omani insurgency. The shift in Saudi policies contributed significantly toward improving the security situation for Oman. In Dhofar, the Rub al-Khali no longer offered a route for supporting the insurgents; instead, the Sultanate and its allies could focus on a far more finite problem — the PDRY border. When the Kingdom convinced the PDRY to withdraw support from the Front, the insurrection totally collapsed.

Saudi Arabia's support ended for two reasons. First, strong Saudi antipathy to communism and concern over the danger posed by radical secular Arab nationalism caused King Feisal to realize that the Sultanate was by far the lesser of evils. Second, the Iranian military presence in Oman became a critical issue. During the 1970s, the primary focus of Riyadh's policy toward the Omani Sultanate was to create a situation in which the Sultanate would feel secure enough to ask Iran to remove its troops and air force units. The introduction of Iranian forces on the Arabian Peninsula was a pragmatic military necessity that contributed toward a decisive change in Saudi policy. This is particularly sobering when looking at the current insurgencies facing the U.S. Although in Oman the number of insurgents was relatively small and the counterinsurgency campaigns were militarily successful, the insurgencies were only eradicated when the external political environment changed and the rebels lost their safe havens. Without the changed political environment, the insurgencies could well have sputtered on almost indefinitely.

Finally, there is the role of ideology. From the beginning of Al Bu Sa'id rule in the mid-18th century, there was an ideological component to Sultanate and Imamate politics that divided the competing centers of power. Throughout most of the 250 years, the Imamate held the upper hand ideologically. This was particularly true in the aftermath of the Canning Award and the overthrow of Imam Azzan bin Qays. As discussed, Imam Qays was probably the only Al Bu Sa'id ruler judged to be worthy of both the titles of Sultan and Imam. The rebellion of 1913 and the near collapse of the Sultanate followed by the Treaty of Sib in 1920 constituted a *de facto* recognition of the social and cultural differences of the Sultanate and the Imamate. The rise of radical neo-Ibadi practice during those years merely served to confirm to its detractors the relative lack of ideological legitimacy associated with the Sultanate. In challenging Sultan Sa'id bin Taymur, the opposition always played the Islamic ideological trump card.

Initially this was true in Dhofar as well, and then the ideological paradigm shifted. In the beginning, the revolt had strong support among many religious conservatives of the principally Sunni region. Sultan Sa'id ruled as a northern Ibadi who was oppressing the Sunni Dhofari population. Two things changed this situation. First, the National Liberation Front founded the PRSY (later PDRY). They and their communist supporters began to drive the Omani Front's policies. Issues like women's rights and other socially unacceptable programs in conservative Dhofari society began to alienate the more conservative members of the Front causing many of the old-line Front members to abandon the organization. The Front's increasing dependence on China and other communist and radical Arab countries pushed policy in Dhofar even further left creating an ideological divide between much of Dhofari tribal society. Then the Front compounded the problem by using draconian enforcement tactics that included the removal of children and executions for those who refused to adhere to the new socialist dogma. These policies provided the Al Bu Sa'id with the Islamic ideological high ground. Whether or not they were "upright Ibadis," the Sultans were obviously not as odious to the local population as the leftists and their supporters. Second, Sultan Qaboos' succession placed a Sultan on the throne who had been born in Dhofar and whose mother was Dhofari. Qaboos shrewdly played his Dhofari heritage. Islam was a trump card in the propaganda campaign that placed the Front squarely on the defensive. In tribal societies in the Middle East and Southwest Asia, it is difficult if not impossible for anyone to win the propaganda war if they find themselves on the wrong side of that Islamic ideological trump card.

As we ended the first decade of the 21st century, a decade marked by two wars in which — as the social, cultural and thus ideological outsiders — the West finds itself clearly losing the ideological war. No matter the intentions, opponents easily portray the Western powers as foreign intruders attempting to impose un-Islamic values on traditional societies. In fact, U.S. success in the Middle East during the Cold War was to a significant degree predicated on our support for conservative Islamic political groups against the communist or secularist non-believers. The insurgencies that are now underway are in countries with populations that number in the tens of millions as opposed to a few hundred thousand like that of Oman during its insurgency period. The insurgents also have the advantage of safe havens. As opposed to the British "less is more," the United States, with its large commitment of military force, has taken ownership of the wars and become the focal point of resistance. Oman and the British also had the perfect alternative leader in the person of Sultan Qaboos. Facing similar issues, the U.S. and its Western allies lack that alternative. If Oman is the example of a successful counterinsurgency effort, then the comparison with the obstacles that the U.S. now faces is not encouraging. Perhaps a return to a smaller special operations war might have better results. In a situation where successful nation building or a conventional military victory is unlikely; a reversion to a special operations war might in fact prevent our adversaries from winning — perhaps the best result that can be achieved. ⬆

Endnotes

1. Benedict Anderson, *Imagined Communities* (London: Verso Books, 2006), 160. Anderson's work is a challenging look at modern nationalism and its effect on global communities. He views it as selling a myth unity to communities whose interests are fundamentally different—the creation of *imagined* communities and argues that the real surprising issue is not that adherents to these imagined communities are willing to kill for a myth but that millions have been willing to die for one. This book is a challenging work but a most interesting look at nationalism. It also provides some thoughts for practitioners of nation building.

2. William Faulkner, *Requiem for a Nun*.

3. Eleanor Gillespie, "Arab Revolt: Could Oman turn into the next Egypt?" *British Broadcasting Corporation* (2 March 201 — http://www.bbc.co.uk/news/mobile/world-middle-east-12616457).

4. Senior Arabian Gulf military officer knowledgeable about Gulf security affairs. When the question: "What happens after Qaboos was posed at the Sultan Qaboos Cultural Center and the Elliott School of International Affairs' Middle East Policy Forum, Washington, D.C.: "Oman 2010: 40 Years — Building the Future," a conference for the 40th anniversary of the accession of His Majesty Sultan Qaboos bin Said on September 30, 2010, the almost uniform response from panelists who would comment was: "That is the big question."

5. Sir Arnold Wilson, *The Persian Gulf: An Historical Sketch from the Earliest times to the Beginning of the Twentieth Century* (London: George Allen &Unwin, Ltd., 1954): 77.

6. Fuad I. Khuri, *Imams and Emirs: State, Religion and Sects in Islam* (London: Saqi Books, 1990): 57. Khuri pointed out that the "same could be said" of the relationship between the "political personality" of Yemen and the emergence of the Zaydis in the ninth century. Despite similarities, both arose out of opposition to the Sunni dominance, both emerged in southern Iraq, and both in theory had elected imams, they come from different traditions — Kharijite and Shi'a. The Ibadi absolutely rejected the belief that the Imamate was limited to the Alid line — descendants of the fourth Caliph Ali. There are other doctrinal differences as well.

7. P.M. Holt, editor, *Cambridge History of Islam, Volume 2B* (Cambridge: The Cambridge University Press, 1970): 592.

8. John C. Wilkinson, *The Imamate tradition of Oman* (Cambridge: Cambridge University Press, 2009): 1.

9. Ibid., 9.

10. Wendell Phillips, *Oman: A History* (London: William Morrow & Company, 1962): 4-7. Phillips believes that something happened to challenge the dominance of the Persians in Oman during the first century but his skeptical of the details of the account provided by al-Kalibi. It is a skepticism that is well justified because al-Kalibi's account contains literary forms that are almost standard to any early Islamic history. In this case, the most pronounced is the Persian use of war elephants

and the account that Malik's sons personally killed the largest. In Isam al-Rawas's *Oman in Early Islamic History* (London: Ithaca Press, 2000): 28-29, the author takes the story accepts the story of the migration as true but dates it in the 2nd century CE with the Sassanian Persians as the occupiers of Oman and Malik's opponents.

11. Phillips, 7. Southern Arabs viewed themselves as descendants of al-Qahtan or Hud. Al-Qahtan was a semi-mythical ancestor who was ethically purer than northern Arabs who descended from Ishmael through Adnan. In the 20th century, the distinction remained important and at times contributed to feuds and political disputes. There is a tendency to downplay these differences in both Yemen and Oman particularly by those against whom it has been used to undermine their political or social legitimacy. Even among those who have historically claimed descent from one of the lines, the claim is often inconsistent with other genealogical claims. Nevertheless, in southern Arabia, most notably Yemen and Oman, various groups have used this distinction to bolster their claims to legitimacy and to undermine their opponents. It reinforces the idea of an exceptionalist identity. See also Manfred W. Wenner, *Modern Yemen 1918-1966* (Baltimore: Johns Hopkins University Press, 1967): 30 and the *Encyclopedia Britannica Online*.

12. Malcolm C. Peck, *Historical Dictionary of the Gulf Arab States* (Toronto: The Scarecrow Press, Inc., 2008), 215.

13. Phillips, 7.

14. Al-Rawas, 38. If indeed, al-Rawas is correct about 'Amr Ibn al-'As, the future conqueror of Egypt, then all likelihood his presence was more persuasive than the letter. While there is some dispute, it makes sense that the Prophet would have sent a competent senior commander. See also, Michael Isaac, *A Historical Atlas of Oman* (New York: The Rosen Publishing Group, Inc., 2004): 18, who also states that al-'As was the messenger.

15. The *Ridda* Wars or wars of apostasy were fought in the immediate aftermath of the death of the Prophet in 632. Many tribes confused the pledge of allegiance to Islam with a personal pledge to Muhammad. They felt absolved of any obligation to maintain their loyalty after the Prophets death. Abu Bakr refused to compromise with the "apostates" and systematically subjugated them. Abu Bakr dispatched Hudhaifa bin Mihsan to quell the revolt in Oman.

16. Phillips, 9. While not on a par with Christianity and Judaism as people of the book, Zoroastrians were often tolerated as intermediate step between the people of the book and paganism.

17. Phillips, 9.

18. Al-Rawas, 111.

19. John Esposito, *The Oxford History of Islam* (London: The Oxford Press, 1999): 35. The Umayyad Caliphate (661-750) dated from the death of the last *Rashiduun* Caliph Ali. Centered in Damascus, its practices created significant opposition particularly in Mesopotamia and Persia. Later another Umayyad Caliphate emerged in Spain. It was overthrown in 750 and replaced by the Abbasid Caliphate (750-1258). The

Sunni Abbasids ruled from Baghdad often under the control of various other political groupings including the Shi'a Buyid family, the Seljuk Turks and others.

20. Patricia Rizzo, *Oman and Muscat: an early modern history* (London: Croom Helm Limited, 1986): 5.

21. Ibadi is a term used by other Muslims to differentiate or label this group. As a rule, Ibadi Muslims reject the label arguing that they represent the true form of Islam and therefore should be referred to as simply the Muslims. This view is reflected in their designation of their imam as the "*imam al-muslimiin*" i.e. the Imam of the Muslims — the implication being obvious. The author is this paper is well aware of both this theological premise and cultural preference, but to provide clarity and simplify writing will refer to the sect as Ibadi, Ibadi Muslims, or Ibadi Islam.

22. Khuri, 107. In simplified form, the Ibadis are that verse Quran 4/100 which states, "He who emigrates in the cause of God in the earth finds many a refuge, wide and spacious. And he who parts off (*yakhruj*) from his home (emigrating) to God and His Messenger, and then dies, his reward becomes due surely to God. God is oft-forgiving and most merciful." The Ibadis argue that by "parting off ... to God" they are by no means departing the Islamic *umma* but instead are merely "rebelling against tyranny."

23. Richard F. Nyrop, *Area Handbook for the Persian Gulf States* (Washington: Foreign Area Studies — The American University, 1977):342.

24. Al-Rawas, 76-77.

25. Al-Rawas, 64.

26. Wilkinson, 205.

27. Phillips, 11. The author explains the issue of tenure for an Imam with the example of the second Imam Sheikh Muhammad bin Abu Affan al Yamadi (793-795). Apparently Abu Affan was "arrogant, tactless and imprudent;" therefore, after two years, the tribal leaders met and elected a new more suitable imam, al-Warith Bin Kaab al-Kharusi 795-808).

28. Wilkinson, 10.

29. Ibid., 11.

30. Ahmed H. Al-Maamiry, *Omani-Portuguese History* (New Delhi: Lancers Publishers, 1982): 1-3. Al-Maamiry states, "Possibly other Arabs such as Yemeni's were also involved in this trade, and if we understand that Omanis came from Yemen, then they were the same Arabs whether referred to as Yemeni or Omani." This is something of an oversimplification. See footnote 18.

31. In many respects, Oman and Yemen shared some interesting developmental similarities. There was the fundamental dichotomy between people of the shore and those of the mountains. On the shore of the Arabian Sea, there was constant interaction and rivalry between groups located in what is now Yemen and Oman. Despite the fact that the Yemeni Imamate was Shi'a and emerged roughly 200 years after that of the Ibadis in Oman, both shared some interesting attributes — namely the idea that the imam was to be chosen by the community based on the best available candidate

and not heredity or some other political criteria. Both were moderate forms of Islam and both Imamates were for the most part centered in the mountainous hinterland. As a result, both were afflicted by the frictions and mutual suspicions that tend to separate shore and mountain people. There were differences as well. In Yemen, agricultural production of the highlands could support a much larger population; thus the demographic center of gravity was in the upland areas of the country. In addition, the Yemen highlands were very much a part of the Hejaz community of commerce and intercourse. The ancient spice routes ran through the highlands and what is now Saudi Arabia into the Levant and Egypt. The case of Oman is significantly different. First, the highlands lacked the agricultural capabilities to support a population that was anything like that of upland Yemen. This meant that the demographic center of gravity was much nearer the coast. Second, with the exception of parts of Dhofar that were tied to the spice trade routes running through Yemen, the mountains of Oman served as a barrier disconnected from the rest of Arabia. When coupled with the *Rub al-Khali* (Empty Quarter) it served to further isolate Oman from the rest of Arabia.

32. Phillips, 24-27.

33. Al-Maamiry, *Omani-Portuguese History*, 5.

34. Nyrop, 342.

35. Ira M. Lapidus, *A History of Islamic Societies*, (London: Cambridge University Press, 1988): 669.

36. R.J. Gavin, *Aden under British Rule* (London: C. Hurst & Company, 1996): 11. In 1280, the Rasulids took control of Dhofar and most of the ports along the Arabian Sea littoral.

37. Patricia Risso, *Merchants and Faith: Muslim Commerce and Culture in the Indian Ocean* (Boulder: Westview Press, 1995): 45-47.

38. Phillips, 31-34. Chroniclers from the period relate stories of atrocity after atrocity including the massacre of Africans Christians who had converted from Islam.

39. John Duke Anthony, *Historical and Cultural Dictionary of the Sultanate of Oman and the Emirates of eastern Arabia* (Metuchen, N.J.: Scarecrow Press, 1976): 81.

40. Phillips, 39.

41. Al-Maamiry, *Oman-Portuguese History*, 30-33.

42. Ibid. 100.

43. Phillips, 40.

44. Ibid., 46-47.

45. Ibid., 51.

46. Wilkinson, 12.

47. Ibid., 53.

48. Phillips, 56, 60.

49. Anthony, *Sultanate of Oman*, 6.

50. Salil Ibn Razik, *History of the Imams and Seyyids of 'Omanfrom A.D. 661 to 1856*, translated by George Percy Badger, FRGS (London: The Hakluyt Society, 1872): 145-155. See also, Rizzo, 41. When Ahmad bin Sa'id made is final move against the Persian forces in Oman, Nadir Shah had withdrawn most of the troops including his commander Taqi Khan. Faced with a far more potent foe, the Ottomans, Nadir Shah needed his forces to confront the threat from the West. As a result, the Persians in Oman became more reliant on their local governors to maintain control and authority and Ahmad bin Sa'id took advantage of the situation.

51. Rizzo, 41.

52. Wilkinson, 13.

53. Rizzo, 44.

54. Phillips, 65.

55. Anthony, 6.

56. Rizzo, 53-65.

57. Ibid., 77.

58. Ibid., 96.

59. Ibid., 101.

60. Ibid., 107.

61. Wilkinson, 13.

62. "Minute from the Foreign Officer Department of Research to the Eastern Department, 24 December 1954," Public Records Office (PRO), FO 371/114578.

63. Madawi al-Rasheed, *A History of Saudi Arabia* (London: Cambridge University Press, 2002): 21-22.

64. "Minute, 24 December 1954," PRO, FO 371/114578.

65. Rizzo, 55.

66. Ibid., 75. See also Christopher Bayly, *Imperial Meridian: The British Empire and the World 1780-1830* (London: Longman, 1989): 55. Bayly discusses in detail the collapse of the decline if not collapse of the great Muslim empires, the Ottoman, the Safavid, and the Mughal and the impact that this had on the rise of British influence and the "peripheral" states of the region of which Oman should be counted as one. He also commented that after the demise of Nadir Shah in 1747 trade with Persia resumed but it was the Dutch who benefited the most.

67. Ibid., 78, 83-84.

68. Phillips, 70-72.

69. Rizzo, 31-33.

70. Wilkinson, 15-16.

71. Rizzo, 33.

72. Phillips, 86.

73. Wilkinson, 228.

74. Phillips, 86, 88.

75. Wilkinson, 228.

76. Nyrop, 242.

77. Wilkinson, 228.

78. Ibid., 229.

79. Ronald Robinson and John Gallagher, *Africa and the Victorians: the Climax of Imperialism in the Dark Continent* (New York: St. Martin's Press, 1961): 43. Omani rule also turned Zanzibar into a lucrative entrepôt for Indian commerce. It represented a new market and Omani familiarity with the British Indian system allowed for an almost seamless transition of Indian merchants in the Zanzibar trade.

80. Ahmed Hamud al-Maamiry, *Oman and East Africa* (New Delhi: Lancers Books, 1979): 63-68.

81. Wilkinson, 229.

82. J.B. Kelly, *Britain and the Persian Gulf, 1795-1880* (Oxford: Clarendon Press, 1968): 538.

83. Ibid., 541.

84. Ibid., 546-551.

85. Ibid., 551, 553, 638, 648, 665.

86. Wilkinson, 13.

87. Ruzayq, "Editor's Preface," 3.

88. Wilkinson, 237-238.

89. Robert GeranLanden, *Oman since 1856: Disruptive Modernization in a Traditional Arab Society* (Princeton: Princeton University Press, 1967): 306.

90. Kelly, 710.

91. Helen Chapin Metz, editor, *Persian Gulf States — Country Studies* (Washington, D.C.: Federal Research Division Library of Congress, 1994): 298. There is a counter-interpretation of Azzan's rule that is more sympathetic to the Sultan branch of the Al Bu Said and the British. The argument is that that the Qays branch of the Al Bu Said in the periodic alliances with Ibadi ulema managed in 1868 to place Azzan bin Qays al-Sa'id in a position where he became the "self-declared imam." While Hinawi tribes supported him, the "public" (whoever that was) "neither elected him nor acclaimed him" as imam. The British viewed his attempt to centralize control over both the coast and interior as a threat to "their established order," and they supported Turki bin Sa'id and the overthrow of Azzan. This version of events lacks the more comprehensive explanations of Kelly and Wilkinson who buttress their arguments about ignorance driving policy with tomes of research.

92. Briton Cooper Busch, *Britain and the Persian Gulf 1894-1914* (Berkeley: University of California Press, 1967): 18. Quote is from: "Report from Consult Mackirdy to Department of State, August 24, 1887, National Archives College Park, Maryland (NACPM), 59, T-638/1.

93. Metz, 298.

94. Busch, 20.

95. J.B. Kelly *Arabia, the Gulf, & the West* (London: George Weidenfield and Nicolson Limited, 1980): 110. According to Kelly, Sultan Faisal could not speak, read or write Arabic. He usually conversed in Gujarati. Judicially his rule was anything but sharia based. The strict Ibadis were incensed that he permitted alcohol and tobacco and allowed Jews, Christians, and Hindus to live in Muscat.

96. Busch, 56.

97. Ibid., 57.

98. H.J. Whigham, *The Persian Problem: An Examination of the Rival Positions of Russia and Great Britain in Persia with Some Account of the Persian Gulf* (London: Isbistor, 1903): 21.

99. Busch, 271-303.

100. Metz, 299.

101. Phillips, 149. Faisal had a pet lion as confirmed by Lord Curzon, the Viceroy of India, and there were reports that he starved it and then used it to execute people. Members of the Sultan's family denied that the lion was the palace executioner. It is difficult to say whether this was an attempt to protect Faisal's reputation or that of the lion; nevertheless, the story illustrates the degree of British involvement because "the lion eventually dies and at a gentle suggestion from the British was not replaced." Faisal was apparently not allowed to choose either his pets or his executioners.

102. Khuri, 57.

103. J.E. Peterson, *Oman in the Twentieth Century* (London: Croom Helm, 1978): 30.

104. Wilkinson, 249.

105. Fred Scholz, *Entwicklungstendenzen in Beduinentum der KleinenStaaten am Persischen/Arabischen Golf – Oman alsBeispiel* (Vienna: Mitteilungen der Oster-reichischenGeographischenGesellschaft, 118, 1, 1976): 89.

106. Wilkinson, 249, 251. Imam al-Khalili was the grandson of Sa'id bin Khalfan al-Khalili, the principal advisor to Sultan and Imam Azzan bin Qays, who had been murdered by Sultan Turki bin Sa'id in 1871. Despite a promise of safe passage and amnesty from Turki's British backers, Turki buried al-Khalili alive. Also see "Report from Major L.B.H. Hayworth, 9 May 1917 and 24 July 1918, British Library Collection, India Office Files, L/P &S/10/427 1913/4684, Parts 3 and 4.

107. Francis Owtram, *A Modern History of Oman: Formation of the State since 1920* (London: I.B. Tauris, 2004): 50.

108. "Minute from Department of Research to the Eastern Department, 24 December 1954," PRO, FO 371/114578: 15-16.

109. Wilkinson, 251. Taken from "Report No. 2052 from Wingate," British Library, IO L/P & S/10/427.

110. Owtram, 62-65.

111. Peterson, *Oman in the Twentieth Century*, 31. Peterson goes on to state, "In many ways, Sa'id was considered by the British as the brightest hope for the Sultanate since Sa'id bin Sultan. Yet it was to be with great relief that they eventually saw him deposed in 1970."

112. Owtram, 79.

113. Ibid. 77, 80.

114. Wilkinson, 287. As Wilkinson commented, "When an exasperated British negotiator exclaimed, 'If the Saudi government always claimed as a Murra [al-Murrah] well the next well beyond the last well we had conceded, there would be no reason why they should not eventually claim Muscat town,' he was stating not more than the reality."

115. Ibid., 289.

116. The coast of the present day UAE was dominated by the al-Qawasim tribal states of Ras al-Khaimah and Sharjah in the 18th century. The Qawasim earned a living from trade, pearling and piracy. The British referred to the coast as the "Pirate Coast." In 1819, the British crushed the Qawasim and in 1853, forced the emirates of the southern Gulf to sign a "treaty of permanent truce" hence the name Trucial States. Between 1971 and 1972, the Trucial States became the UAE.

117. Ibid., 292.

118. "Brief on the Saudi Arabian Frontier Dispute for the United Kingdom Delegation to the United Nations, 18 April 1953," PRO, FO371/104294, EA1081/518.

119. P.S. Allfree, *Warlords of Oman* (London: Robert Hale, 1967): 14-17. Allfree provided the following description of the potential opposition to the Saudi incursion: "The only forces at the disposal of the Sheikh of Abu Dhabi were his own armed tribesmen; those at the fingertips of the British Government, which was supposed to be the Protector of the areas, were a small local military police force of some fifty men stationed in Sharjah under a British gentlemen commander; the representative of Oman had a handful of bellicose but ineffective ceremonial guards." Allfree described the TOL as "gangs of discharged soldiers from Aden were dug out of the back streets and freighted up to Sharjah ... there was more than a fair share of criminals ... [and] they had not the slightest interest in whether Turki or the Sultan of the Sheikh of Abu Dhabi lived or died, and they owed no allegiance whatever to the Political Agent. There was not a great deal ... of legitimate loot. They had one commodity which they could sell for good cash to their supposed enemies ... their ammunition." Stories about the TOL in the early days of the Buraimi problem rarely surfaced because they did not generally fit with the heroic view offered later. See also, Peter Clayton, *Two Alpha Lima* (London: Janus Publishing Company, 1994): 16. Clayton explains that the TOL was entirely a British creation formed for "the maintenance of peace and good order in the Trucial States and providing an escort for the British Political representatives." Michael Mann in The Trucial Oman Scouts (London: Michael Russell, 1994): 19, states that the Trucial Omani Scouts, the later name for the TOL, tended to be *bedu* and were paid for and trained by the British and therefore at the beck and call.

120. Senior Arab military officer knowledgeable about tribal issues. He stated that the credit for healing the breach between the tribes and the Emirates following the British expulsion of the Saudis from Buraimi was due to intelligence of Sheikh Zaid bin Sultan al-Nahayan (1918-2004) of Abu Dhabi and the respect with which he was viewed by the interior tribes.

121. J.E. Peterson, *Oman's Insurgencies: The Sultanate's Struggle for Supremacy* (London: SAQI, 2007): 54-55.

122. "Brief, 18 April 1953," PRO, FO371/104294, EA1081/518.

123. AvrahamSela, *The Continuum Political Encyclopedia of the Middle East* (New York: Continuum International Publishing Group, 2002): 659.

124. Allfree, 15.

125. "Brief, 18 April 1953," PRO, FO371/104294, EA1081/518.

126. "Brief, 18 April 1953," PRO, FO371/104294, EA1081/518.

127. Ibid.

128. "Brief, 18 April 1953," PRO, FO371/104294, EA1081/518. Apparently there was some disagreement in Riyadh among the Omanis. When the Omani group returned via Bahrain to Oman, Suleiman bin Himyar stayed behind for further talks. The returning group had two requests of the British in Bahrain: "(i) to arrange to have Suliman bin Hamyar [sic], who was in Riyadh at the time, poisoned on his way home. (ii) to recognize travel documents issued by the Imam who, they claimed, was independent." No doubt the British in Bahrain would have liked to comply with the former and were troubled by the latter. The Saudis were obviously supporting the old claim of independence on the part of the Imamate vis-à-vis the sultanate.

129. Ibid.

130. "Briefing Paper from the Eastern Department/Arabia: The Sultan of Muscat and the Interior of Oman, 1 May 1953," PRO, FO371-104294, EA1081/519/G.

131. Allfree, 15.

132. "Minute to the FO from A.D.M. Rose (Muscat) on Conversation with Sultan Sa'id, 9 March 1953," PRO, FO371/104278, EA1081/206. The Sultan was also concerned with the defection of Suleiman bin Himyar who was in Riyadh and stated that he had ordered him to be killed as soon as possible.

133. Wilkinson, 295.

134. "Minute Discussing the Sultan's attitude toward the HUQF Project, 26 January 1954," PRO, FO371/109829, EA1081/49. See also, "Telegram from FO to the British Residency Bahrain, No. 91, 27 January 1954," PRO, FO371/109829.

135. "Dispatch on Meeting with Sultan Sa'id from Bahrain to FO (Eden), No. 14, 4 February 1954," PRO FO371/109829, 10815/51/54.

136. Wilkinson, 298.

137. Ibid., 304, 308.

138. Owtram, 91.

139. "Dispatch from the British Residency Bahrain to the FO/Eastern Department (Fry) on Saudi Activities, 26 October 1954," PRO, FO371/114613, EA1081/603.

140. "Dispatch from the British Residency Bahrain to the FO on Oman and the Arab League, 1 April 1955," PRO, FO371/114578, EA1015/S. The dispatch or letter was a suggestion that Sultan Sa'id offer his own views to the Arab League but the Sultan refused. In "Telegram from Bahrain to the FO on the Arab League Issue, No. 2, 18 January 1955," PRO FO371/114578, EA1015/8, the Sultan pointed out that he had made is position clear. First he did not recognize the Arab League and second any outcome in Cairo was be prejudiced from the start; therefore as he had said before he was not going to respond.

141. Wilkinson, 315.

142. Macmillan's Diary, May 6, 1953, Macmillan Papers, Bodleian Library, Oxford University. Also quoted in Harold Macmillan, *Tides of Fortune, 1945-1955* (New York:Harper & Row, Publishers, 1969): 502-503. On the eve of the Dulles trip, Harold Macmillan groused that in addition to Jefferson Caffery, the U.S. Ambassador in Cairo giving "aid and comfort" to the Egyptians, London would now have to contend with Dulles. "In Egypt, there is to be an interval [in the Anglo-Egyptian negotiations] for a fortnight. No doubt the Egyptians (who already rely on the American Ambassador Caffery) ... are hoping to get something out of Dulles, who is due to arrive in a day or two. ... Dulles is sure to make a 'gaffe' if it is possible to do so." It is interesting that Dulles first major trip through the Middle East and South Asia coincided with a "crisis" in Anglo-American relations. See also, "Who Likes Dulles — Who Doesn't," Newsweek (27 January 1958): 28. The British disliked and distrusted Dulles intensely. They believed that he was responsible for excluding them from the ANZUS Treaty. They saw him as "too rigid" and detested his moralizing. Dulles and Churchill liked the limelight. Bridling at the competition, Churchill allegedly stated, "I am told that on Mondays, Wednesdays, and Fridays, Mr. Dulles makes a speech. And that on Tuesdays, Thursdays, and Saturdays, he holds a press conference. And that on Sundays he is a lay preacher. With such a regimen, there is bound to be a certain attenuation of thought."

143. "Telegram from Dulles in Baghdad to Eisenhower, May 17, 1953," Dwight David Eisenhower Library (DDEL), Presidential Papers of DDE (PPDDE), Anne Whitman File (AWF), Dulles-Herter Series, Box 1: 1. An Interview with William C. Lakeland, Berkeley, California, 23-24 September 2003 sheds additional light on British frustration with the situation in Cairo. Much to the chagrin of the British, the American embassy in Cairo had already interposed itself as the "go-between" for Anglo-Egyptian negotiations. American Ambassador Jefferson Caffery used his relationship with British Ambassador Sir Roger Stevens and the relationships between Caffery's political officer William Lakeland, Muhammad Heikal, and Nasser himself to gain a bird's eye view of the negotiations. Lakeland became the intermediary carrying versions of the agreement back and forth between the Egyptians and the British. See also, Roby C. Barrett, *The Greater Middle East and the Cold War: US Foreign Policy under Eisenhower and Kennedy, 1958-1963* (London: IB Tauris,

2007), where the Introduction contains a discussion of the Anglo-American rivalry and the difficulty that London had in adjusting to the new reality of global power.

144. "Telegram from FO to Berlin on Saudi Arabia Frontier Dispute, No. 179, 11 February 1954," PRO, FO371/109829, EA1087/80.

145. "Telegram from FO to Berlin on Saudi Frontier Dispute, No. 180, 11 February 1954," PRO, FO371/109829, EA1087/80.

146. "Letter from British Residency Bahrain to FO on Muscat and Oman issues, 23 April 1955," PRO, FO371/114578, EA1013/1/101/55.

147. "Letter from the FO to the British Residency in Bahrain on Muscat and Oman issues, 11 May 1955," PRO, FO371/114578, EA1015/21.

148. Majid Al-Khalili, *Oman's Foreign Policy: Foundation and Practice* (Westport, Connecticut: Praeger Security International, 2009): 24.

149. Ibid., 25.

150. Allfree, 21-25. Because of a mutiny and other mayhem caused by the TOL recruits from Aden, the decision was made to replace all the Adenis with local loyal tribal levies so that by the time of the action against the Saudis and their allies at Hamsa, the TOL consisted of local troops and British officers.

151. "Telegram from Bahrain to the FO on Buraimi situation at nightfall, No. 765, 26 October 1955," PRO, FO371/114623, EA1081/336.

152. "Telegram from Bahrain to the FO on Buraimi situation, No. 766, 27 October 1955," PRO, FO371/114623, EA1081/336.

153. "Telegram from the Commonwealth Relations Office Prime Minister Eden's speech, No. 270, 26 October 1955, PRO, FO371/114623.

154. "Telegram British Embassy Jidda to the FO Saudi position on Buraimi, No. 290, 28 October 1955," PRO FO371/114578, EA1081/357.

155. Peterson, *Oman's Insurgencies*, 77. See also, Clayton, *Two Alpha Lima*, 178, in which he states that three Buraimi sheikhs were captured and deported by the British85— Sheikh Sagar bin Sultan, Sheikh Bin Hamad, and the son of Sheikh Abid bin Jammah.

156. Al-Khalili, 25-26.

157. The so-called calm in Oman during 1956 probably had as much to do with the Suez Crisis and the turmoil over the contrived Israeli, British, and French attack on Egypt as any other factor. In fact, there are indications that the extremely negative reaction of the United States and the Eisenhower administration to the tripartite attack on Egypt was due at least in part to Washington's unhappiness over British actions at Buraimi against Saudi Arabia the year before. Eisenhower basically demanded a British, French and Israeli withdrawal from Suez and began to undermine the British and French currencies to obtain it.

158. Peterson, *Oman's Insurgencies*, 78-80.

159. Peterson, *Twentieth Century*, 185.

160. Youssef Choueiri, *Arab Nationalism: A History – National and State in the Arab World* (London: Blackwell Publishing, 2001): 204.

161. Peterson, *Oman's Insurgencies*, 81.

162. Ibid., 82-83.

163. Ibid., 84.

164. Peterson, *Oman's Insurgencies*, 85. Al-Khalili in *Oman's Foreign Policy*, 29, states that the British hesitated to provide support because of the tide of rising Arab nationalism, the debacle over Suez the year before, and Washington's continuing displeasure, as related by Secretary of State John Foster Dulles, with "the rather belligerent attitude of the British along the Arabian Sea, particularly in relation to Oman." The British under the new government of Harold MacMillan certainly attempted to coordinate better with Washington but, in matters of the Gulf, both London and Washington agreed that was an area of British responsibility. During the period, 1956-1958, the British made it clear that they believed the debacle at Suez was the fault of Dulles who had once again misled them. The British reaction in Oman in 1957 was a foregone conclusion and the request for assistance from the Sultan was orchestrated by them in the sense that they told the Sultan that he had to make a formal request to get the assistance that he needed. The opening line of the Sultan's request, "You have full knowledge of the situation," points to the fact that the British officers in the OR and other Omani commands including the Chief of Staff had already made it clear that direct British intervention would be required to rectify the situation. Al-Khalili does an excellent job describing the frustrations and frictions between the U.S. and Britain from 1953 to 1958.

165. Ibid., 85-86.

166. Ibid., 87-90. The surrender of Birkat al-Mawz caused a problem among the British. Apparently Major Dennison of the MAF and Peter Chubb of the TOS inadvertently entered the town ahead of Lieutenant Colonel Carter's column. The town offered its surrender and they accepted. Carter was livid because he had arranged an elaborate filming of his entry and the surrender as a capstone to the campaign and Dennison and Chubb ruined it.

167. Ibid., 89.

168. Al-Khalili, 29.

169. Suzanne St. Albans, Duchess of St. Albans, *Where Time Stood Still: A Portrait of Oman* (London: Quartet Books: 1980): 91. Al-Khalili in *Oman's Foreign Policy*, 31, quoted Colonel Smiley reporting from Muscat on the use of U.S. mines: "The ideal answer, of course, would have been for us to stop the mines at source, in other words to persuade the Americans either to stop supplying them to the Saudi Army or to exercise some control over their use. ... the Americans were brutally unsympathetic. Their reply was that they supplied the mines to Saudi Arabia under their military Aid Program, and it was not their concern how the Saudis chose to employ them."

170. Peterson, *Oman's Insurgencies.*, 95.

171. Ibid., 96. See also reporting on the March Plan in "Telegram Situation Report from HQ/MEAF to the Ministry of Defense London, 24 March 1958," PRO, PREM 11/2402.

172. "Minute from the FO Eastern Department to Prime Minister Macmillan, 28 April 1958," PRO, PREM 11/2402.

173. Peterson, *Oman's Insurgencies*, 100.

174. "Minute on Operation Dermot in Oman from Eastern Department, 11 August 1958," PRO, FO371/132524, BA1015/93.

175. Peterson, *Oman's Insurgencies*, 110-112. See also Al-Khalili, *Oman's Foreign Policy*, 48-51. The author discusses another element that could be attributed to the hardening of British resolve namely the Omani enclave of Gwadar on the Pakistani coast. The Sultanate had held Gwadar since the late 18th century. Pakistani independence brought repeated requested for negotiations aimed at removing Sultanate control. At the height of Talib bin 'Ali's incursion and the Jabal al-Akhdar crisis with the Imamate, the British told Sultan Sa'id that if he did not sell Gwadar to Pakistan that in all likelihood Pakistan would just take it and the Sultan would get no compensation at all. London also informed Sa'id that in the event of a Pakistani move on Gwadar, he could expect no help from H.M.G. This incident underscored the increasing British frustration with Sa'id's seeming inability to adjust to the new realities around him. In this case, the Sultan finally acquiesced and sold Gwadar to the Pakistani government. 110-113.

176. Ibid., 121, 126.

177. Ibid., 135. The British mounted a real effort to discover some Soviet weapons or munitions on the mountain top "as this might have a tremendous effect on public opinion in the United States."

178. Ibid., 139. Most of the munitions and heavy weapons were of U.S. manufacture although there were a few Soviet mines. The U.S. weapons came to Oman via Saudi Arabia.

179. Kelly, *Arabia*, 118.

180. Peterson, *Oman's Insurgencies*, 187. In *The Making of the Modern Gulf States* (Reading: Ithaca Press, 1998), 130, Rosemary Said Zahlan stated, "The Sultan, desperate to maintain the new unity of Oman, appealed to Britain for further assistance. In so doing, he lost sight of his earlier objective to make Oman independent." It is far more likely that Sultan Sa'id never lost sight of that goal however he put the survival of his regime first. Neither Sa'id nor Imam Ghalib were capable of creating anything that approached a modern functioning state both wanted a Sultanate or Imamate as the case may have been isolated from the rest of world and frozen in time. Neither vision had any real chance of surviving; only the Sultanate had any hope of bridging from a pre-modern tribal society and political construct to a paradigm that could survive in the late 20th century and has a chance of surviving in the 21st.

181. Peterson, *Oman's Insurgencies*, 185.

182. Maamiry, *Oman and East Africa*, 114.

183. DilipHiro, *TheEssential Middle East: A Comprehensive Guide* (New York: Carroll & Graf Publishers, 2003): 389.

184. Al-Khalili, 55-56.

185. "Text of the broadcast propaganda from the Sawt al-Arab in Cairo on Oman, 26 August 1958," PRO, FO371/132524, BA1015/106, in which Mahmud Id, a member of the Association for Political Science, stated, "The period we live in is marked by a gigantic struggle against this imperialist tyranny [the British]. ... The period we live in is marked by the spread of the spirit of Arab nationalism in the area. There is a strong tendency moving the Arab people in the Gulf and South [Aden] to join up with their brethren in the other Arab countries. ... After imperialism has tried to incapacitate them by depriving them of their resources and draining their blood, but the free people have raised the siege, stepped out of the cordon of isolation imposed by the imperialists and come out to the head of the sacred march. ... Examples of these free rulers are the Imam of Oman ... [and] Sultan Ali Bin Abd al-Karim, the Sultan of Lahj." The Sultan of Lahj was a tribal leader in what was then an area of the British Western Protectorate in South Yemen and is now the Lahj province of Yemen. In 1958, he defected with his British-armed tribal forces to the cause of Imam Ahmed in Yemen. It was a major embarrassment to the British. It should also be noted that Lahj is one of the centers for the southern separatist movement in Yemen today and also an area of operation for Al-Qaeda in the Arabian Peninsula (AQAP). This is a good case in point for the idea of a never ending insurgency.

186. Owtram, 121-122.

187. Peterson, *Oman's Insurgencies*, 187.

188. Ibid., 188-193. The term *jabili* pronounced *gabili* in Yemen and Oman comes from the word *jabal* or mountain — literally meaning a person from the mountains. It can be used in a very pejorative way much like the term "hill billy" in English.

189. Maamiry, 115.

190. Peterson, *Oman's Insurgencies*, 193.

191. Maamiry, 115.

192. Peterson, *Oman's Insurgencies*, 193.

193. Ibid., 196.

194. Ibid., 197. The Saudi-Egyptian honeymoon had cooled in 1961 when the Syrians staged a coup and abruptly withdrew from the UAR, and turned to open hostility when Egyptian trained and supported Yemeni officers staged a coup in September 1962 and created the Yemen Arab Republic (YAR). Given that the Saudis were furnishing the Yemeni Royalists with weapons and funds to kill Egyptian soldiers in Yemen and *Sawt al-Arab* was once again labeling the Kingdom a feudal state, Saudi-Egyptian cooperation on Oman had virtually ceased. With Nasser now a pariah, the Saudis turned to Iraq and its violently anti-Nasserist leader, Abd-al-Karim al-Qasim. This also problematic because

when Kuwait achieved its independence in 1961 Qasim claimed it as the 19th province of Iraq and threatened to invade. In 1963, a coup destroyed Qasim's government and cost the Iraqi leader his life. He was replaced by Abd-al-Salaam al-Aref, an Iraqi nationalist, in a coalition with the Ba'athists. Aref had originally be jailed for being too pro-Nasserist. The upshot of all this external turmoil was that there was a singular lack of trust and coordination on the part of the DLF's supporters that made the life in the DLF much more complicated.

195. Barrett, Roby, *Yemen: A Different Political Paradigm in Context*, (Tampa: JSOU Press, 2011). In the 1970s, the government in South Yemen changed its name from the PRSY to the Peoples' Democratic Republic of Yemen, the PDRY.

196. "Report from Muscat (Carden) to British Residency Bahrain (Luce), 15 January 1966," PRO, FO371/185363. Quoted in Al-Khalili, 123.

197. Peterson, *Oman's Insurgencies*, 202-203, 211.

198. Peter Thwaites, *Muscat Command* (London: Leo Cooper, 1995): 74.

199. Maamiry, *Oman and East Africa*, 116-117.

200. Peterson, *Oman's Insurgencies*, 218.

201. Maamiry, *Oman and East Africa*, 116-117.

202. Ibid., 215-217.

203. Ibid., 218-225.

204. Ibid., 229.

205. Hiro, 389.

206. Maamiry, *Oman and East Africa*, 117-118. The Ba'th Party had partnered with Abd-al-Salaam al-Aref in his overthrow of the Qasim government in Baghdad in February 1963. One of the core groups supporting Qasim had been the Communist Party of Iraq (CPI) which the al-Aref's nationalist, Nasserist and Ba'thist supporters utterly destroyed. Thus, the name may have been the Arab Ba'th Socialist Party but they were anything but pro-communist, and the new Iraqi Ba'th hoped to exploit the British withdrawal from the Gulf without being subsumed in a broader movement dominated by the Chinese and Soviets and their clients. As a result, they supported this independent movement in the north that sought a repeat of 1957.

207. Ibid., 119.

208. Peterson, *Oman's Insurgencies*, 233-234.

209. Ian Skeet, Muscat and Oman, the end of an era (London: Faber and Faber, 1974), 201.

210. Calvin Allen, Jr. and W. Lynn Rigsbee II, *Oman under Qaboos: From Coup to Constitution, 1970-1996* (London: Frank Cass Publishers, 2002): 28.

211. Ibid., 238-241. A search of the palace revealed large stocks of weapons and ammunition including tear gas grenades put aside for this very eventuality. Apparently the Sultan who was not in his private apartments could not get access to them.

212. Allen, *Oman under Qaboos*, 29. See also Ian Gardiner, *In the Service of the Sultan: A First Hand Account of the Dhofar Insurgency* (London: Pen & Sword Military,):

23 in which the author points out that Sultan Sa'id had displaced his own father in a coup and suggests that "it may have been a relief for the old man."

213. Peterson, *Oman's Insurgencies*, 243. Al-Hirthi's code name was "Ashtray."

214. Major General Tony Jeapes, BD, OBE, MC, SAS *Secret War: Codename Operation Storm* (London: Harper Collins Publisher, 1996): 30.

215. Ian Gardiner, *In the Service of the Sultan: A first-hand account of the Dhofar insurgency* (Barnsley, England: Pen & Sword Military Books, Limited, 2006): 74. In most of the accounts written by SAS officers, the term "*adoo*" or "*adu*" is used to describe the insurgents or Front fighters. "*Adoo*" (*adu*) simply means an enemy in Arabic.

216. Ibid., 246.

217. Ibid., 229, 249.

218. Ibid., 253, 267.

219. Maamiry, 119.

220. Peterson, *Oman's Insurgencies*, 267. The move to consolidate is most interesting because Peterson credits Ali Salim al-Bayd, the supervisor of the conference and a leader in the PRSY's NLF, as the key driver behind the strategy. Ironically, al-Baid emerged as the leader of the Peoples' Democratic Republic of Yemen (PDRY), the new name for the PRSY, when it eventually unified with the Yemen Arab Republic in 1990 to from the new unified Republic of Yemen. He then led a revolt and separatist movement against the Yemeni government dominated by northerners. He lost and had to flee to Oman where for a period of time he was given asylum. So eventually he returned to Oman but not in the role that he had envisioned in 1971.

221. Hiro, 390.

222. Peterson, *Oman's Insurgencies*, 278-280.

223. Ibid., 288-294.

224. Ibid., 296.

225. Peter Radcliffe, *Eye of the Storm: Twenty-Five Years in Action with the SAS* (London: Michael O'Mara Books Limited, 2000): 81.

226. Peterson, *Oman's Insurgencies*, 298.

227. Jeapes, *SAS Secret War*, 145.

228. Peterson, *Oman's Insurgencies*, 300.

229. Jeapes, *SAS Secret War*, 156.

230. Peterson, *Oman's Insurgencies*, 301-302.

231. Ibid., 308.

232. Ibid., 319.

233. Ibid., 325.

234. Ibid., 333.

235. F. Gregory Gause III, *Saudi-Yemen Relations: Domestic Structures and Foreign Influence* (New York: Columbia Press, 1990): 128. Gause stated that Iranian troops in Oman ignited Saudi paranoia on multiple fronts -- ideological, ethnic, sectarian, and regional geopolitics. In the context of the times, Pahlavi Iran was a focus of suspicion and competition.

236. Ibid., 356-357, 380-381.

237. Ibid., 391.

238. *The Revolution is Alive in Oman: The Liberation Struggle in Oman* (Denmark: KROAG, 1979): 46-52.

239. Allen, *Oman under Qaboos*, 63.

240. Allen, *Oman under Qaboos*, 48-56.

241. R. HrairDekmejian, "Forging Institutions in the Gulf Arab States," Iran, Iraq and the Gulf Arab States, edited by Joseph A Kechichian (New York: Palgrave Publishers, 2001): 308.

242. Sultan Qaboos bin Sa'id Al Sa'id, *Basic Law 1996*, Article 5.

243. Sultan Qaboos bin Sa'id Al Sa'id, *Basic Law 1996*, Article 6.

244. Judith Miller, "Creating Modern Oman," *Foreign Affairs* (May/June 1997): 17.

245. Allen, *Oman under Qaboos*, 220.

246. Ibid., 225-226.

247. Ibid., 217.

248. Ibid., 61.

249. A western military officer knowledgeable about Omani affairs.

250. Mark N. Katz, "Assessing the Political Stability of Oman," *Middle East Review of International Affairs*, 8, No. 3 (September 2004): 3.

www.ingramcontent.com/pod-product-compliance
Lightning Source LLC
Chambersburg PA
CBHW081840280526
45789CB00007B/2514